SACRAMENTO PUBLIC LIBRARY

3 3029 04250 4852

D0761166

ECTION OF
LIBRARY

JTER

SACRAMENTO, CA 95023

2/03 (1)

1/01

Library of
AFRICAN-AMERICAN HISTORY

Farewell to Jim Crow

THE RISE AND FALL OF SEGREGATION IN AMERICA

R. KENT RASMUSSEN

☑® Facts On File, Inc.

Farewell to Jim Crow: The Rise and Fall of Segregation in America

Copyright © 1997 by R. Kent Rasmussen

All rights reserved. No part of this book may be reproduced or utilized in any form or by any means, electronic or mechanical, including photocopying, recording, or by any information storage or retrieval systems, without permission in writing from the publisher. For information contact:

Facts On File, Inc.
11 Penn Plaza
New York NY 10001

Library of Congress Cataloging-in-Publication Data

Rasmussen, R. Kent.
    Farewell to Jim Crow : the rise and fall of segregation in America/
        R. Kent Rasmussen.
        p. cm. — (Library of African-American history)
    Includes bibliographical references and index.
    ISBN 0-8160-3248-3
    1. Afro-Americans—Segregation—History—Juvenile
literature.
    2. Afro-Americans—Civil rights—History—Juvenile literature.
    3. United States—Race relations—Juvenile literature. I. Title. II. Series.
E185.61.R237 1997
305.896'073—dc21   96 0048329

Facts On File books are available at special discounts when purchased in bulk quantities for businesses, associations, institutions, or sales promotions. Please call our Special Sales Department in New York at 212/967-8800 or 800/322-8755.

You can find Facts On File on the World Wide Web at http://www.factsonfile.com

Text design by Cathy Rincon
Cover design by Nora Wertz
Illustrations on pages 37, 89, 127 by Jeremy Eagle

Printed in the United States of America

MP FOF 10 9 8 7 6 5 4 3 2

For Kathy, who shares the anger

Grateful acknowledgment is given to Gwendolyn L. Rosemond for permission to print an extract from her essay that first appeared in Ann Taylor, ed., *Shaping the Short Essay* (New York: HarperCollins, 1990). Most of the illustrations in this book are courtesy of the Library of Congress, Prints and Photographs Division.

Contents

Preface

The Romans used the Latin verb *segregare* to describe separating parts of their livestock from the rest of their flocks and herds. That word later found its way into English to give us *segregate* and *segregation*. These modern English words have much the same meaning as their ancient Latin forebear, but they are now used mainly in reference to forced separation of human beings from one another. Examples of human segregation range from the harmless division of public restrooms into men's and women's bathrooms to the repressive confinement of Native Americans to reservations. Most often, however, the term is applied to the forced separation of black Americans from white Americans.

In almost every imaginable situation that draws people together, white Americans have devised forms of segregation to exclude African Americans. Some forms have been established by government, others by private institutions and citizens. Some have evolved spontaneously, more or less by voluntary, mutual consent. In all these forms segregation has affected how African Americans could travel and where they could lodge; where they could live, work, go to school, and worship; and where they could shop, eat, and amuse themselves. Whatever its origins, however, segregation has always had the destructive effect of keeping black and white Americans ignorant and suspicious of each other.

American segregation reached its high-water mark in the middle of the 20th century. Since the mid-1950s, African Americans have waged a relentless battle to eliminate all vestiges of segregation, and they made desegregation a central goal of the modern civil rights movement.

The central theme of this book is the process of desegregating American society; however, the book's purpose is not simply to retrace ground well covered in countless works on the civil rights movement. To appreciate segregation's complex rise and fall, it is necessary to examine its deeper history in the centuries-long African-American quest for equality. This historical approach will reveal that while desegregation has been a goal of African-Americans, it has not always been the most important one. Indeed, a central irony in African-American history has been the fear that many white Americans have had that "race mixing" is a paramount goal of black people. If anything, the opposite has been the case. As with almost all peoples in all times, what African Americans have most wanted has been no more and no less than equal justice and opportunity. Desegregation is a key to this goal, simply because it is impossible for anyone to enjoy fair opportunities while the confining barriers of segregation remain.

1

A Strange Idea: How Segregation Worked

In early 1940 actress Hattie McDaniel received an Academy Award for her memorable performance in Gone With the Wind—*a film that many Americans rank as the greatest ever made. When the film had opened two months earlier in Atlanta, the state of Georgia celebrated the premiere as a grand holiday. Clark Gable, Vivien Leigh, and other cast members were welcomed like royalty as they entered the theater to watch the film. McDaniel and certain other cast members, however, were not invited.*

◆

Several years later, not far from Atlanta, American soldiers escorted German prisoners of war from one internment camp to another. Along the way, they stopped at a roadside café for lunch. While the enemy soldiers were fed at tables inside the café, their American guards were handed their food at a back door and told to eat outside.

◆

These strange incidents illustrate the peculiarities of a once widespread social institution known as segregation—the physical separation of people according to their skin color. The reason that actress Hattie McDaniel did not attend her own film premiere was that she was black and the theater showing her film admitted only whites. Likewise, the café that welcomed enemy soldiers inside while excluding American soldiers did so because the Germans were white and the GIs were black. Grotesque as these incidents were, they represent the kinds of treatment that most African Americans took for granted in their daily lives before the 1960s. Those who have grown up since then have doubtless experienced discrimination, but nothing remotely resembling what earlier generations faced.

Americans have practiced many forms of racial and ethnic segregation in their history, but none so pervasively and for so long as that which they imposed on African Americans. The segregation of black people developed slowly during the colonial era, when slavery was the lot of most African Americans. After American independence, segregation increased in the Northern states, where slavery was mostly abolished. After the Civil War and Reconstruction, segregation reached its height, where it became a way of life in the South.

By the 20th century, the expression "Jim Crow" (see box) had become a synonym for the various institutions of segregation. Jim Crow rules limited almost every aspect of African Americans' lives: where they could live, study, work, play, and worship; how they could travel; and even where they could be jailed or buried. "White Only" and "No Colored" signs pervaded the South, and they were far from unknown in the North. They appeared in public buildings, bus and train stations; barber shops and beauty salons; hotels, restaurants, stores, theaters, and hospitals; and at swimming pools, playgrounds, parks, and beaches. At its most basic level, however, segregation was imposed invisibly; many African Americans lived in unlabeled but virtually all-black neighborhoods—particularly in the North. Outside of the South white neighborhoods needed no "white only" signs to inform African Americans that they were not welcome.

The government's placement of a Jim Crow drinking fountain directly in front of a North Carolina courthouse seems to raise questions about the nature of the justice dispensed within. (Courtesy Library of Congress, Prints and Photographs Division)

"Jim Crow"

Throughout the 20th century the name *Jim Crow* has meant segregation of African Americans. Jim Crow railway cars, buses, and elevators were those reserved for African-American passengers; Jim Crow restaurants and hotels were those for black guests; Jim Crow park benches and drinking fountains were for black pedestrians; and so on. More broadly, however, *Jim Crow* (or *jimcrowism*) has come to mean the entire structure of segregation and all its ugly manifestations.

Exactly how this name came to be associated with segregation may be impossible to determine. Informal, everyday language, being essentially oral rather than written, rarely lends itself to precise historical reconstruction. Even in modern times new expressions enter the language and gain wide popularity before anyone can pinpoint their origins.

Various attempts to trace the origins of *Jim Crow* disagree on details; however, a few things can be said with some confidence about the expression's early history. During the 1820s and 1830s a white entertainer named Thomas D. Rice ("Daddy" Dan Rice in some accounts) gained renown by performing mock African-American musical routines in blackface make-up. Minstrel shows, as routines such as Rice's were known, were a popular form of entertainment that arose in the South and found avid audiences through the United States well into the 20th

In the most visible manifestations of Jim Crow—particularly in the South—public buildings had separate "white" and "colored" entrances, separate service counters, separate restrooms, and separate drinking fountains. Separate telephone booths and even separate elevators were not uncommon. Thirsty Southerners often bought their soft drinks from separate vending machines or from machines with separate coin slots for black and white customers. Some courthouses were known to keep separate Bibles on which black and white witnesses swore their oaths during trials, and warehouses stored school textbooks for white and black century. Featuring white performers with their faces painted black, such shows contributed significantly to white stereotypes of African Americans as slow-witted clowns who were naturally inferior.

Around 1830, when Rice was performing in Louisville, Kentucky, he introduced a lively routine to his repertoire called either "Up, Jim Crow" or "Jump, Jim Crow." According to some accounts, Rice copied the routine from a young African-American boy whom he had observed singing a song about "Jim Crow." Typical of racially stereotyped minstrel-show routines, Rice's Jim Crow number featured an ignorant black man who performed exaggerated physical antics. The popularity of his act doubtless helped to associate the name *Jim Crow* with black inferiority.

The earliest known use of *Jim Crow* to describe segregation was recorded in Massachusetts in 1841, when it was applied to a separate railway car for black passengers. The use of the term so soon after Rice popularized it suggests a connection between his song and the expression's sociological meaning. However, how the term *Jim Crow* came to be used in a sociological context can be only guessed. It is possible that both Rice's song and the segregation term borrowed the name *Jim Crow* from some now forgotten use of the words that developed *before* Rice made the expression famous. Such details are not, however, as important as the fact that *Jim Crow* gained currency as a synonym for segregation. By 1900 it was a common term for any racially segregated facility ◆

pupils separately—even if the books themselves were the same.

African Americans could not escape from segregation even in death. Indeed, cemeteries have been among the most rigidly segregated institutions in America. Even among religious denominations that were unusually tolerant of nonwhites, strict segregation in burial arrangements was often the rule. American cemeteries were not always segregated, however. During the days of slavery, black servants were often buried in the plots of their masters' families. After the Civil War, however, some whites moved the remains of some of these people to all-black cemeteries, helping to ensure that the nation's dead remained even more segregated than the living. Even dead pets have been segregated according to the colors of their owners.

Segregation assumed some of its classic forms in public transportation. Few sectors of everyday life offered more vividly public evidences of color lines. When African Americans went to their segregated homes, schools, and hotels, they were out of the sight of their white counterparts. Public transportation was different; it forced segregation to the surface. In the South, Jim Crow buses once required African Americans to sit in rear seats—a form of physical segregation too obvious to go unnoticed. Jim Crow trains likewise carried both white and black passengers—but in separate cars—with those carrying blacks typically placed just behind the filthy, smoke-belching locomotives. Train stations and bus terminals in the South almost always had highly visible Jim Crow waiting rooms, ticket windows, and restrooms.

Jim Crow facilities at a Georgia railroad station (Courtesy Library of Congress, Prints and Photographs Division)

Modern air transportation escaped Jim Crowism. By the time that the air-passenger industry was in full swing, federal laws against segregation in interstate transportation worked against the development of segregated seating on both international flights and domestic flights—most of which were governed by federal laws on interstate travel.

The African-American war against Jim Crowism in public transportation began early in the 19th century, and it was waged mostly in the North. Throughout the midwestern, eastern, and New England states, black urban dwellers had to fight daily battles to get around in the cities by streetcars and other means of conveyance. After Reconstruction (1866–77), the South became the area of the greatest fights against segregation in public conveyances. A landmark Supreme Court decision affirming that segregation was legal under the U.S. Constitution was *Plessy v. Ferguson* (1896). It concerned segregated seating arrangements on a Louisiana train. The "separate but equal" principle came out of this Court decision, and had a profound impact on the country for a half century. It not only governed segregation in public transportation throughout the South, it was extended to justify segregation in other spheres, including education.

To avoid the indignities of traveling on Jim Crow trains and buses, African Americans preferred to make long trips in private automobiles whenever possible. The availability of relatively inexpensive automobiles since the 1920s greatly helped to liberate Southern African Americans from Jim Crow transportation. In 1940 a sociologist observed that the public highway was a place where rules of segregation were suspended. "Effective equality," he wrote, "seems to come at about twenty-five miles an hour or above. As soon as the car is stopped by the side of the road, to pick wild flowers or fix a puncture, the color of the occupants places them in their traditional racial roles."

Automobile travel presented special segregation problems of its own. Sooner or later motorists had to stop—to refuel

Sign such as these were rare but welcome sights for African-American motorists in South Carolina. (Courtesy Library of Congress, Prints and Photographs Division)

their cars, relieve themselves, eat, or find places in which to sleep overnight. White motorists have always counted on meeting these simple needs wherever they stop; not so African Americans.

By the mid-20th century, almost every American community of any size had at least one hotel, motel, or boardinghouse to accommodate travelers. In communities too small to support more than a few such public accommodations, the likelihood was that they were restricted to whites. Difficulties in finding overnight accommodations in unfamiliar towns made long-distance automobile travel an uncomfortable and occasionally perilous undertaking for African Americans. Black travelers often found alternative informal accommodations in private homes in small communities. To avoid complications, African Americans often completed long car trips without stopping to rest overnight. The strain of driving great distances with inadequate rest occasionally had tragic results. In 1950, for example, Dr. Charles R. Drew, a distinguished physician who pioneered the study of blood-typing (and crusaded against segregating medical blood supplies), undertook an overnight drive from Washington, D.C., to Tuskegee, Alabama. He died from

Jim Crow facilities at a bus terminal in Louisville, Kentucky (Courtesy Library of Congress, Prints and Photographs Division)

injuries that he received after falling asleep at the wheel and crashing.

Restaurants, like public accommodations, historically catered to travelers; in Jim Crow country they also tended to practice rigid segregation. Although eating meals has never had the same social significance in the United States that it has in other countries, social taboos against black and white people eating together have been among the strongest forces for segregation in America. Until passage of the federal civil rights acts of the 1960s, virtually all public eating places in the South were legally segregated. Older civil rights laws of many Northern states banned discrimination in public

*From Virginia to Florida it was
a nightmare. There was no place
for us to eat or sleep on the
main highways. Restaurants
wouldn't serve us . . . Some
gasoline stations didn't want to
sell us gas and oil. Some told us
that no rest rooms
were available.*

◆

—Mahalia Jackson,
Movin' On Up (1966)

restaurants, but African Americans could rarely count on being served anywhere outside their own communities. Although few people would rank being served in restaurants as important as voting or receiving good educations, the humiliations that African Americans suffered in Jim Crow eating places gave opposition to this form of segregation special symbolic significance.

One of the most consequential social legacies of the 20th century may prove to be the residential segregation of American cities. After African Americans began migrating out of the South during the 19th century, the residential areas of most Northern cities into which they moved fragmented into racially distinct neighborhoods. In almost every city, whites lived in the most expensive and desirable neighborhoods, while blacks—along with immigrants and other minorities—were confined to the most depressed and least desirable areas. Much of this urban segregation was de facto, in that it evolved naturally in response to economic factors and the common human preference to live among people with whom one is socially comfortable. The segregation of urban African Americans has, however, been far from voluntary. Aside from the limitations on where they could *afford* to live (thanks in large part to discriminatory hiring practices that restricted their incomes), African Americans were kept out of better neighborhoods by both discriminatory laws and private white resistance.

Where residential segregation was not legally mandated, it was often fostered by private business practices, especially in the North. During the first two decades following World

War II, private agreements known as restrictive covenants controlled access to about 90 percent of the new housing units built in the country. These covenants were pledges that white homeowners signed promising never to sell their property to members of designated racial or ethnic groups. The exclusions of any given covenant typically applied to non-white groups—who were variously labeled "Negroes," "Arabs," "Indians," "Mongolians," and so forth. The covenants occasionally excluded non-Christian whites—especially Jews. The language of covenants could be confusing. For example, a West Virginia covenant that barred Ethiopians from buying property required a court test to establish that "Ethiopians" meant *all* black persons. In general, however, African Americans did not need court tests to determine whether restrictive covenants excluded them. They always did.

The rationale behind restrictive covenants was the argument that if white neighborhoods allowed black people to move in, property values would plummet. Comedian Dick Gregory ridiculed this logic. Looking for a house can be "quite an experience," he said, "especially when you go to a white neighborhood, offer $40,000 for a $23,000 house, then get turned down 'cause you'd be lowering the realty values."

Although restrictive covenants were private contractual agreements, they usually had the force of state law behind them. In 1926 the U.S. Supreme Court ruled that the covenants were not unconstitutional. About two decades later, the Court began to reverse this decision, but it would not be until the sweeping civil rights legislation of the 1960s that the federal government stood squarely behind the principle of nondiscrimination in housing. Meanwhile, covenants occasionally had absurd results. For example, a District of Columbia court once refused to let a white property owner sell his covenanted property to blacks, even though the property itself was surrounded by black families. The court said that the fact that the property was surrounded by African Americans did not necessarily make it "unfit" for white occupancy. Following that line of reasoning, one might wonder why the restrictive covenant was necessary in the first place.

Whatever its root causes, residential segregation has been the single most important underpinning of segregation generally. Segregation in housing has reinforced the segregation of schools, churches, social organizations, shops, public entertainments, and amusements. As a result, even in cities that have tried to desegregate their schools, the segregation of residential neighborhoods has worked against those efforts; it often negates the positive effects of desegregation or makes school desegregation an unachievable goal.

Segregation in employment has manifested itself in both the workplace and in the distribution of jobs. Until the late 19th century most African Americans worked in agriculture, a fact that limited their employability in other areas. The

The shabbiness of this rural café was not uncommon several generations ago; however, its "colored only" sign is a grim reminder of government-imposed segregation. (Courtesy Library of Congress, Prints and Photographs Division)

country's rapid economic development during that same period created millions of jobs in industry, but most of these went to new European immigrants, and white trade unions generally excluded African Americans from membership. In factories in which African Americans were allowed to work, they were typically assigned to the least desirable and lowest paying jobs. In the South factories that hired African Americans almost always segregated their workers—in separate wings or even in separate buildings. Most of this kind of segregation was not sanctioned by law, but South Carolina enacted a law requiring Jim Crow entrances, Jim Crow pay-ticket windows, Jim Crow stairways, Jim Crow restrooms, and other Jim Crow facilities in its textile factories.

Even the federal government was not immune to segregating workers. President Woodrow Wilson stunned his African-American supporters in 1913 by issuing an executive order to segregate the restrooms and eating facilities used by federal civil servants.

Segregation took an especially heavy toll on black professionals. Segregated educational institutions limited the opportunities of African Americans to train in fields such as law and medicine. Those who did became lawyers and doctors then faced further discrimination in finding employment, joining professional associations, and building up clientele. Black lawyers, for example, were long excluded from membership in the American Bar Association; they had difficulty winning equal standing in courtrooms; and they were even handicapped by a widespread preference among fellow African Americans to engage white lawyers. Black doctors and dentists suffered from similar handicaps and faced the additional hindrance of placing patients in hospitals in which they themselves could not practice their professions. Both African-American laborers and professionals typically reacted to such discrimination by forming their own trade unions and professional organizations.

One of the most unpredictable arenas in which segregation was practiced was commercial establishments. Aside from rules founded on local laws and customs, the extent to which any given business practiced segregation had to do with such matters as how much contact its customers had with one another, what competition the business faced, and how much it could profit from African-American patronage.

During the late 1930s the Swedish sociologist Gunnar Myrdal conducted extensive research into the condition of African Americans; he published his findings in 1944 in *An American Dilemma: The Negro Problem and Modern Democracy*. He observed that segregation tended to be practiced least where services were most impersonal—as in gas stations. At the other end of the spectrum, however, he found almost complete segregation in personal-service establishments, such as barber shops and beauty salons, in *both* the North and the South. Between these extremes there were unpredictable variations from community to community. Practices among department stores, for example, varied widely. Some, for example, would serve African Americans, but not allow them to try on clothes or to exchange their purchases. The bewildering variations among commercial establishments that Myrdal observed included Southern stores that discriminated less against black customers than their Northern counterparts did.

To avoid the embarrassment and restrictions of shopping in white establishments, many African Americans preferred to patronize places operated primarily for black customers —even if they were not owned by African Americans. Mindful of discriminatory hiring practices, African Americans avoided places that did not hire black employees. Around 1930 a quiet "don't buy where you can't work" campaign arose throughout the country.

Throughout the nation's history, the military has been an important arena for testing desegregation. Until the Vietnam War—the first in which America's armed forces were thoroughly integrated—every major U.S. military conflict raised the question of whether African Americans should fight and if they should be segregated from white troops. Despite the fact that every war demonstrated both the fighting ability of black troops and at least some success in using racially integrated units, each succeeding conflict seemed to forget the lessons of its predecessor. This was particularly true at the beginning of the Civil War, when Union politicians and military leaders resisted the idea of recruiting and arming African Americans to fight, despite the fine combat records of integrated units in the Revolutionary War and the War of 1812. The Civil War began the system of organizing segregated military units on a large scale. The practice continued through World War II and was not ended until after President Harry S Truman issued an executive order abolishing segregation in the military in 1948.

No institution of modern American society is more thoroughly segregated than its churches. Both historical and political reasons account for this phenomenon. Toward the end of the colonial era, as increasing numbers of African Americans sought membership in churches, they discovered that the principles of Christian brotherly love rarely discouraged white parishioners from refusing them full fellowship. White churches either excluded blacks from membership altogether, or they forced them to accept segregated seating arrangements and other humiliations. Refusing to accept inequality in houses of God, African Americans soon discovered that forming their own churches gave them places where they could gather in relative freedom from white control. They built their churches into powerful centers that provided community leadership, mutual support, entertainment, and more. From the early 19th century, membership in Christian churches was rigidly segregated and it has largely remained so. Development of rigid residential segregation reinforced the pattern of segregated churches—even in

Northern cities whose white churches stood ready to welcome black members. In contrast to other institutions, white churches have had little to offer to African Americans that could be regarded as superior to what black churches provide, so long as their members prayed to the same God and aspired to reach the same heaven.

Equal access to education is such a crucial element of democracy that the extent to which it exists can be a measure of equality in the society as a whole. Since the early 19th century, access to education has been a central African-American concern, which even at the end of the 20th century remains an elusive goal for many blacks. A key obstacle to equal education has been, and remains, segregation. At one time or another segregated public schools existed in every region of the United States. The segregation of public schools grew along with the rapid development of public educational systems in the late 19th century. By the mid-20th century, all the Southern states, the District of Columbia, and parts of other states maintained completely separate elementary and secondary school systems for white and black students. Individual cities in some Northern states also mandated at least partly segregated systems, and in most other big cities residential segregation effectively kept the public schools segregated.

Although the Supreme Court's 1896 *Plessy* decision applied to a transportation case, the "separate but equal" principle that it formulated was later widely regarded as a constitutional justification for segregated schools. The failure of segregated school systems to live up to their own separate-but-equal philosophy eventually doomed them. Through unrelenting legal challenges to the inequalities in Jim Crow school systems, African Americans eventually persuaded the Supreme Court to overturn the very principle of separate but equal.

Among other rigidly segregated 20th-century institutions have been places of amusement, especially in the South. In most Southern states all entertainments patronized by white

In the days of Jim Crow, going to a movie usually meant two things to African Americans: They would most likely have to sit in a balcony, and they might have to enter the theater from the rear. (Courtesy Library of Congress, Prints and Photographs Division)

people were either off-limits to African Americans or were physically divided into white and nonwhite sections. White dance halls, swimming pools, bowling alleys, skating rinks, and the like excluded black people altogether. Even the nation's capital segregated its theaters and other amusements. Southern theaters and assembly halls that did not exclude blacks invariably relegated them to the poorest seats. In many cities the Jim Crow balconies of movie houses were known as "nigger heaven." In some cities African-American groups that hired assembly halls for meetings arrived to find themselves locked out of the restrooms and other facilities. To avoid having to deal with such treatment, blacks often used their own churches for secular meetings and entertainments—a practice that further contributed to the important role of churches in black communities.

Major-league professional sports have seen most of their growth since the mid-20th century, around the same time that the barriers of segregation began to fall. Until Jackie Robinson joined baseball's Brooklyn Dodgers in 1947, however, professional sports were the exclusive preserve of white athletes—even though no major-league teams in any sport were then based in the Jim Crow South. Segregation in college sports reflected the patterns in the colleges and universities themselves. Prior to the integration of Southern campuses in the early 1960s, no black athletes played for any Southern colleges except the traditionally black schools. White Southern universities even avoided scheduling games with Northern universities to spare their athletes from having to compete against African Americans—a practice that also helped to preserve a belief in white athletic superiority.

Under a constitutional government such as that of the United States, courts play a crucial role in administering justice and settling private disputes. For social and political equality to be a reality, all citizens must have equal opportunities to conduct lawsuits, testify as witnesses, sit as jurors, and attend trials as observers. Throughout much of U.S. history, however, access to the courts was far from equal. African Americans were typically barred from testifying—especially against whites—and many states would not allow them to serve on juries. Such discrimination made their struggle for equality even more difficult because it was largely in the courts—not legislative bodies—that they sought recognition of their rights.

Perhaps the ultimate form of discrimination within a democracy is denying members of a group the right to share in decision-making by not letting them vote. Discriminatory voting laws are not, strictly speaking, forms of segregation; however, the one cannot be understood without reference to the other. The history of African-American voting rights reads like a barometer of segregation in the United States: Almost everywhere that African Americans have been able to vote freely, legal segregation has melted away. The process of desegregation began in earnest during the post–Civil War Reconstruction era when large numbers of Southern blacks could vote; it went into full retreat after Reconstruction, when new voting laws meant to keep blacks away from the polls were enacted. Desegregation began again in the 20th century, as the federal courts and U.S. Congress restored black voting rights.

Since Great Britain began colonizing North America in the early 17th century, African Americans have been the group that suffered most severely from segregation. However, the damage done by segregation has never been limited to blacks. Segregation has wasted the resources of American society as a whole, by retarding the development and utilization of a large portion of human talent. Segregation has required expensive duplication of facilities and services and made life more cumbersome and complicated for everyone—black and white.

Segregation did far more than merely inconvenience and annoy its victims; it even endangered their lives—by limiting their access to timely medical care and by forcing them to travel farther and under worse conditions than they otherwise would have had to in order to accomplish ordinary tasks. Furthermore, people who violated segregation rules—intentionally or not—risked insults, beatings, or worse from angry whites.

Everywhere that segregation has been practiced, it has increased social hostility and tension, and it has made a mockery of the democratic and egalitarian principles on which the nation was founded. The contradiction between American democratic principles and actual practice became even more evident in the 20th century, when the United States assumed a leadership role in the world struggle against non-democratic governments. It was no coincidence that the federal government finally began breaking down the barriers of racial discrimination and segregation in the midst of

America's mid-20th-century cold war against world communism. It simply was not possible to champion freedom and democracy abroad while denying it to a large group of citizens at home.

One of the arguments once used to defend segregation was that it let members of each group "know their place." This was never as simple as it might sound. People of purely northern European descent and people of purely sub-Saharan African descent, for example, might appear to themselves and to others as members of distinct "races"; however, racial types are rarely "pure" and modern scientists continue to debate the very meaning of race. By the 1950s the federal government and the governments of more than two dozen individual states had laws defining "race." These definitions varied so much that some persons who were recognized as legally "white" in one state might find themselves legally "black" in another. In states where people were subjected to institutionalized segregation, the significance of how a person was classified under such laws extended beyond restrictions on where one could eat or sleep or travel to restrictions on where families were allowed to live, where children could attend school, and even who one could marry. In many states there were laws against interracial marriage. Thus, a man and woman married under the laws of a state that classified both as white might find that their marriage violated the laws of another state, which classified one of them as nonwhite and one of them as white.

Individual states typically differentiated between persons judged to be "full-blooded" African Americans (who were usually classified as "Negroes") and African Americans of mixed heritage ("mulattoes"). In contrast, other states classified as Negro anyone who had any trace of African-American ancestry, however slight. Some states wrote specific fractions into their racial definitions. Maryland and Indiana, for example, once defined a Negro as any person with at least one-eighth African ancestry. A person who had only one-six-teenth African ancestry was thus legally white in Maryland and Indiana, but Negro in many other states.

While the mathematics of racial definitions in these now-defunct state laws may have seemed reasonable to those determined to keep the races separate, in practice it was difficult to categorize individuals. Determinations of who was white and who was black often had more to do with the ways in which individuals were seen by others than with actual ancestry—which for people of mixed backgrounds was difficult to document.

In a society in which the prevailing view was that anyone who was not "pure white" was something quite different and inferior, there was often no middle ground for people of mixed heritage. To choose to be one was to deny being the other. Unfortunately, the brutal realities of racial segregation often forced people into making painful choices. In most parts of the country the difference between being legally white and legally black was the difference between having many choices and having few.

In addition to separating people from one another, Jim Crowism gave rise to elaborate systems of racial etiquette that governed almost every aspect of contact among black and white Americans. Everywhere that African Americans went—in the North as well as the South—they had to be alert to local variations in etiquette. Wherever Jim Crow signs were not prominently posted, they were uncertain about whether they were welcome to enter the restaurant, public restroom, or even elevator in question. Getting around in unfamiliar places could be a perilous business. As an old folk song intoned:

> They say if you's white
> you's all right;
> If you's brown,
> stick around,
> But as you're black,
> mmm mmm, brother, git back, git back, git back!

The key to understanding the resistance of African Americans to segregation is appreciating their desire to share the same freedoms and to enjoy the same choices as all other Americans. In fighting for equality for themselves, they have played leading roles helping to define the civil rights and liberties to which everyone is entitled. Their struggle has thus improved the lives of, not only minority groups, but all Americans.

NOTES

p. 7 "Effective equality . . ." Quoted in Gunnar Myrdal, *An American Dilemma: The Negro Problem and Modern Democracy* (New York: Harper and Bros., 1944), p. 1368, n. 50.

p. 11 "quite an experience . . . " Dick Gregory, *From the Back of the Bus* (New York: Avon, 1962), p. 76.

2

Colonial Settlement
and Segregation

African-American history began in Virginia. The first British settlement in North America was only 12 years old when 20 Africans joined the settlers at Jamestown in 1619. Shortly afterward, additional Africans, as well as black South Americans, began to arrive in Jamestown, as well as in the other new British colonies that stretched along the Atlantic seaboard.

Records surviving from Virginia's early colonial years are not sufficiently rich to reconstruct the colony's entire social history. However, what evidence does exist provides tantalizing hints about Virginia's first black settlers. The earliest recorded name of an English-speaking African American was that of a free Virginian named Anthony Johnson. Although slave systems had flourished for a century in the older Spanish and Portuguese colonies to the south, most of Virginia's first black settlers appear not to have been slaves. They evidently arrived as indentured servants. The distinction between indentured servants and slaves was significant. Like the many European immigrants who paid for their passage to America by indenturing themselves as servants, indentured black Virginians would have been obligated only to work for fixed periods for the masters who bought their contracts. Afterward they probably expected to enjoy the same freedoms as other formerly indentured colonists. Unfortunately, this apparent social equality among the first black and white settlers did not long endure.

During Virginia's early years, there was too much work to be done in building the colony and too few settlers to do the work to leave much time for thinking about such matters as racial distinctions and segregation. The later development of segregation would be largely a product of economic changes and rapid population growth. Through the rest of the 17th century, the populations of the British colonies grew slowly but steadily. By 1715—nearly a century after Virginia's founding—Britain's North American colonies counted 434,000 residents, of whom about 59,000, or 13.5 percent, were black. The next seven decades were a period of almost explosive growth. By the time the colonies freed themselves of British rule in 1783, their total population had risen to almost 4 million people. The rate of growth in the African-American population through this period was even greater. At independence, about 750,000 Americans—19 percent of the new nation's total population—were black. This 12-fold increase in African-American residents brought with it many changes that would have consequences far into the future.

Early Virginia's great need for labor planted the seeds for future social and legal distinctions among racial groups. These distinctions in turn gave rise to modern segregation. As the Virginia colony grew during its first half century, the demand for labor to clear the land, work farms, erect buildings, and provide specialized crafts and services outstripped the supply of free laborers. Throughout this period, the numbers of both indentured and free black Virginians increased. Meanwhile, however, the colony institutionalized chattel slavery—a system in which masters owned their workers outright and regarded their slaves as personal property, to do with as they wished. To meet its growing labor needs, the colony turned increasingly to importing slaves from Africa.

Although Virginia's first-known laws pertaining to slavery were recorded only in 1661, most of the colony's 2,000 black residents were chattel slaves a decade later. By the end of the century about 1,000 Africans were being imported into Virginia each year. Until the Civil War began in 1861, the overwhelming majority of African-American Virginians were slaves. The situation was similar in Britain's other colonies in what later became known as the American South.

The introduction of slavery into North America brought with it the idea that color and social condition were related. Because virtually all white residents were free and most blacks were enslaved, skin color soon became a convenient badge of social status. The ability to identify slaves by their appearance made controlling their movements easier: Until proven otherwise, light-skinned people were presumed to be free, and dark-skinned people were presumed to be slaves. The rationale behind legislation and customs designed to control the movements of slaves would later be used to create laws and customs to control free blacks as well.

Until the final years of the colonial era, no part of Britain's North American colonies was entirely free of slavery; however, the institution was never as important in the North as it was in the South. Slaves were being imported into Boston at least as early as 1638, but the Northern economic systems never developed the same need for their unskilled labor that arose in the South. The prevalence of small-scale farming in

Throughout the colonial era most African Americans were slaves who could be bought and sold like any other commodity. (Courtesy Library of Congress, Prints and Photographs Division)

the North mitigated against making economic use of slaves. Meanwhile, however, many Northern merchants prospered from the transatlantic slave trade and played a large role in supplying the Southern colonies' demand for labor. By the early 18th century a mere fifth of all North American slaves were in the Northern colonies.

The rationale behind slave codes was the perceived need to protect white people from the growing number of blacks. As slave systems grew larger, and as occasional slave uprisings increased white fears, the slave codes grew more elaborate and strict. In general, the codes rested on several principles: Slaves were property and not persons; they had no legal standing in the courts; and they should constantly be subordinated in order to get as much work from them as possible. Virtually all the rules of the codes were negative, that is, they restricted something, and many of them contained the roots of later segregation laws. The codes restricted slaves' movements; they limited the ability of slaves to hire themselves out, engage in commerce, or otherwise conduct themselves as free people; they restricted contact among slaves and white people; they forbade slaves from gathering together in groups; and they forbade slaves from learning to read or to possess literature that might cause them to question slavery.

Despite the relatively smaller number of slaves in the North, laws governing slavery there were often as harsh as those in the South. For example, New York and New Jersey, which had the largest Northern slave populations, also had some of the harshest slave codes. A major turning point in race relations in the Northern colonies occurred in 1712 when New York slaves rose up against their masters in one of the largest rebellions of the era. Fear of further revolts moved the colony's government, not only to tighten its slave codes, but to burden free African Americans with new legal restrictions. New York, for example, barred African Americans from owning property. The colony lifted this restriction in 1730, but New Jersey—which had followed New York's earlier example—retained the restriction through the remainder of the colonial era.

Throughout most of the colonial era, laws and social conventions governing relations among black and white people had less to do with race than with conditions of servitude. However, as supporters of slavery began advancing the idea that Africans were mentally and morally inferior to Europeans, racial distinctions were used to justify slavery. From the pulpits of Christian churches, clergymen preached that God sanctioned the enslavement of black people because of their degraded condition. In the face of arguments such as that, race—rather than mere condition of servitude—became a crucial measure of social status. For this reason, the social philosophies behind customs and laws designed to control slaves were increasingly used to restrict African Americans who were not slaves. This kind of thinking was rich ground on which to raise arguments in favor of racial segregation.

As color and social-class distinctions came to mean the same things, new laws arose to govern race relations. As early as 1640 the colony of Virginia punished a black woman and a white man for associating with each other. In 1664 Maryland became the first colony to enact a law prohibiting black men from marrying white women. Concern about the growth of a class of free African Americans can be seen in growing restrictions on the freeing of slaves, beginning in Virginia in 1691. The 18th century brought even more limitations on the civil liberties that free African Americans had previously enjoyed.

One of the great ironies of race relations in America was that black and white people lived in closer proximity to each other, and in greater intimacy, in slave-owning segments of society than in those areas where slavery was uncommon. Under slavery, residential segregation was rarely an issue. Slaves themselves could rarely choose where they lived, so whites had little need to make rules about housing. Slaves generally lived on the property of their owners—usually in dwellings built near their masters' homes, and sometimes even under the same roofs. When masters and slaves shared the same houses, the slaves were likely to be quartered in cellars or in attic garrets. Originally, this kind of physical separation was not necessarily related to racial differences; similar housing arrangements had long characterized master-servant relations in European households.

As the physical property of their owners, slaves were regarded as an intimate part of the household. The nature of the work that slaves did brought them into frequent and close contact with their white masters. Field slaves, for example, typically worked under the direct supervision of their owners, and they rarely ventured far from their owners' property. Almost every aspect of their lives was closely governed by their masters. Domestic slaves had even closer relationships with their masters. They spent most of their working hours inside their masters' homes. In New England colonies, they occasionally even ate at the same tables with their white owners. Domestic slaves prepared and served their masters' meals, cleaned their homes, sewed and repaired their clothes, tended—and sometimes even wet-nursed—their children, tended their masters when they were sick, and generally performed whatever services their masters required. In order to perform such duties, it was essential that slaves reside as *close* to their masters as possible.

Physical distances between the living quarters of masters and slaves tended to grow larger as the numbers of slaves connected with individual households increased. On Southern plantations with dozens of slaves or more, field slaves were quartered in complexes of small houses some distance from the "big houses" of their owners. Separate housing was also common on New England farms with large numbers of slaves. Too much distance between slaves and masters, however, would have been impractical. In contrast to free-labor systems, in which salaried employees are motivated to work by wages and fear of losing their jobs, slave systems depended on compulsion. Employers of free labor need not worry about their employees running off when they are out of their sight—so long as other people looking for jobs are available to replace them. Slave owners, however, could not count on their workers' desire to stay. The need to keep slaves from shirking their duties or running away required owners to maintain close and constant control over every aspect of their workers' lives. This, in turn, made it necessary for slaves to live close by, so they could be watched.

Questions of purely racial segregation during the era of slavery pertained far more to free African Americans than to slaves. In colonies with large slave populations, many white people feared that free African Americans might unsettle the slave communities—either through their example as free men and women, or as agitators for social change. Slave owners naturally reasoned that if their slaves saw other African Americans enjoying the benefits of freedom, they might get the idea that they too could be free. As long as slaves associated their condition of servitude with being black, they could be taught never to aspire to being free. Thus, slave-owners did not want their slaves to have direct contact with free African Americans, whose very existence proved that black people were not inevitably destined to be slaves. Many social institutions that would later become associated with segregation arose from the need of fearful whites to define the status of free blacks during the era of slavery.

Within most colonies the total number of free blacks was too small for African-American communities to be perceived as a threat that required special controls. By the end of the colonial era, fewer than 8 percent of all African Americans were free. The impulse rigorously to segregate blacks from whites was largely a post–Revolutionary War development growing out of the abolitionist movement in the North that accompanied independence. However, while institutions of segregation awaited the early 19th century, its seeds can be seen in many colonial-era institutions.

One of the primary impulses that prompted the British colonization of North America was the quest for religious freedom, particularly among Christians who did not wish to be part of the dominant Church of England. The Protestant Dissenters known as Pilgrims who settled Massachusetts, for example, left Britain for that reason. Likewise, many Roman Catholics left Protestant-ruled Britain hoping to find greater freedom to practice their beliefs in Maryland. In view of the quest for religious freedom that brought many Christians to

North America, it is ironic that American churches themselves eventually became one of the most profoundly segregated sectors of American society.

Few, if any, Africans brought to America as slaves were Christians before they arrived, at least other than nominally. During the 17th century there was considerable uncertainty in the British colonies about whether it was legal for baptized Christians to be slaves. This uncertainty discouraged many slave owners from allowing their own slaves to receive religious instruction, because slave owners did not want the legal status of their slaves to be jeopardized. Around 1700 this issue was resolved when colonial religious leaders, legislatures, and courts decided that a person could indeed be both a slave and a Christian. Once that decision was made, slave owners actively encouraged their slaves to convert to Christianity. Very likely, the slave owners' new motives mixed genuine altruism and self-interest. Some of these people doubtless eased their own consciences about owning slaves by allowing their slaves to enjoy whatever comforts the gospel might bring them.

Many slave owners probably did care about the souls of their slaves; however, many likely looked upon Christianity rather cold-bloodedly as an ally. By encouraging slaves to accept their lot humbly, the churches reinforced the idea that God approved of black slavery and that slaves should look for their rewards, not in their earthly lives, but in heaven.

During the 1700s, the second century of the colonial era, most slaves in North America became Christians, and they generally attended the churches of their masters. Many even attended services in the company of their masters. However, this practice was not necessarily an example of Christian brotherly love; it was a means for slave masters to maintain close supervision over their property. Whites had the sense to realize that if they allowed their slaves to attend separate black churches, such churches could become potentially dangerous centers for black resistance to white domination.

Slaves and Christianity _____

While the earthly lives of slaves might have been wretched, Christian slaves believed that they could look forward to freedom in heaven. Indeed, the hopes of slaves for a better life in the next world inspired black gospel songs such as "There Is a Land of Pure Delight":

There is a land of pure delight,
Where saints immortal reign.
Infinite day excludes the night,
And pleasures banish pain.
There everlasting Spring abides.
And never-with'ring flowers:
Death, like a narrow sea divides
This heav'nly land from ours.
Sweet fields beyond the swelling flood,
Stand dress'd in living green;
So, to the Jews, old Canaan stood,
While Jordan roll'd between. ◆

It was a long time before whites accepted the idea of African Americans attending any kind of religious services at which whites were not present.

When slaves attended white churches, they usually sat in the galleries or in special sections. However, it is now difficult to know whether white churches created this separation because of a conscious desire to segregate the races or because of an even older British tradition of separating the social classes in church. Regardless of motives, however, this practice set a precedent for racial segregation that would endure. In some churches, the white members even erected physical partitions to separate themselves from the slaves. In addition to being seated in separate sections in the churches, African Americans were often subjected to other forms of discriminatory treatment, such as not being permitted to approach the communion tables until after whites had been served.

Probably the nearest thing that black and white people came to experiencing religious brotherhood occurred in the lower South, where long camp meetings and church services were common in Methodist and Baptist denominations. In the North, where most of the colonial era's free blacks resided, African Americans were generally permitted to attend predominantly white churches, but they were rarely admitted to full membership. This was true even in Quaker churches, some of whose white members played leading roles in the movement to abolish slavery. The widespread failure of early American churches to accept African Americans into full membership would bring about dramatic changes early in the independence era and have long-lasting consequences.

The 20th-century crusade to integrate public schools through the court system was at the center of the modern movement to desegregate American society. The kind of state-supported public education that has existed in the 20th century was, however, unknown during colonial times. Such schools as then existed were mostly privately run, typically by churches or missionary groups, with vast differences in facilities among the various colonies. As a consequence, the history of admission of African Americans to these schools was closely connected to the history of the churches themselves. Like much of early African-American history, these issues were closely tied to the history of slavery.

As a general rule, it can be said that within colonial slave societies, whites regarded educating slaves as wrong. It was thought to be to the advantage of slave owners to keep slaves ignorant of everything that their duties did not require them to know. Ideas were regarded as especially dangerous, and the key to the spread of ideas is literacy. Many colonies passed laws making it illegal to teach slaves to read. So long as slaves remained ignorant of alternatives to their condition of servitude, they could be held more easily in subjection.

The American quest for freedom from Britain at the end of the 18th century prompted the first great challenge to the institution of American slavery. Many white colonists who wanted to break away from British rule recognized that it was hypocritical to argue about the natural rights of man as a justification for independence from Britain while at the same time denying these very rights to slaves. This contradiction was not lost on many slaves, either. In Massachusetts, for example, slaves petitioned the General Court for their freedom as a "natural right." In contrast to most other British colonies, which did not allow slaves to institute suits in court, Massachusetts gave its small slave population the opportunity to demand that their masters show by what right they held title to their slaves. While these early legal experiments had only a modest effect on freeing slaves, they set a precedent for establishing the importance of the courts in acknowledging the rights of African Americans. After the colonies became independent, the efforts of African Americans to assert their rights through the courts would play a major role in the new nation's entire constitutional development.

NOTE

p. 32 "There is a land . . ." Quoted in Eileen Southern, *The Music of Black Americans* (New York: W. W. Norton, 1971), p. 88.

3

"[Almost] All Men Are Created Equal": Early Nationhood

After Britain's North American colonies won their independence in the Revolutionary War, they joined together to form the United States—a nation founded on principles of liberty, equality, and justice. Indeed, their Declaration of Independence stated unequivocally that "all Men are created equal, that they are endowed by their Creator with certain unalienable Rights," including "Life, Liberty, and the Pursuit of Happiness." In the struggle against Britain to attain these goals, many American patriots were acutely aware of the contradiction of demanding liberty for themselves while denying it to others. Some argued loudly that the goal of liberty for the nation was inseparable from that of freedom for all people—including African-American slaves. The argument was a strong one, and one that certainly did not escape the attention of African Americans themselves. However, it did not win out. When the new nation was organized, the question of abolishing slavery was left to the individual states.

Most Northern states outlawed slavery during or shortly after the war for independence, but independence itself did not bring about sudden improvements in the condition of most African Americans. Their general condition worsened before it got better. Through the new nation's first century the central issue concerning African Americans was what their status should be. As long as they remained slaves, there were few questions about their rights—for they had almost none. Once they were free, however, difficult questions arose: Were they American citizens? Did they have the same rights as whites? If not, what rights did they have?

African Americans rarely waited for whites to answer these questions for them. Whenever they could, they seized opportunities to petition school boards, city councils, legislatures, and the courts to grant them the rights that they believed were theirs. As early as 1780 free blacks in Dartmouth, Massachusetts, petitioned the Massachusetts General Court for relief from taxation because they were denied the privileges of citizenship. In 1791 free blacks in Charleston, South Carolina, protested to the state legislature about legal inequities—particularly their inability to testify in court or to institute legal suits. Although the protests of most African Americans during that era were rejected, African Americans never stopped demanding their rights.

During the new nation's first 80 years, the status of free African Americans was complicated by the fact that most blacks remained in bondage. Although slavery persisted only in one portion of the country, it had a profound effect on the rights of free African Americans throughout the entire coun-

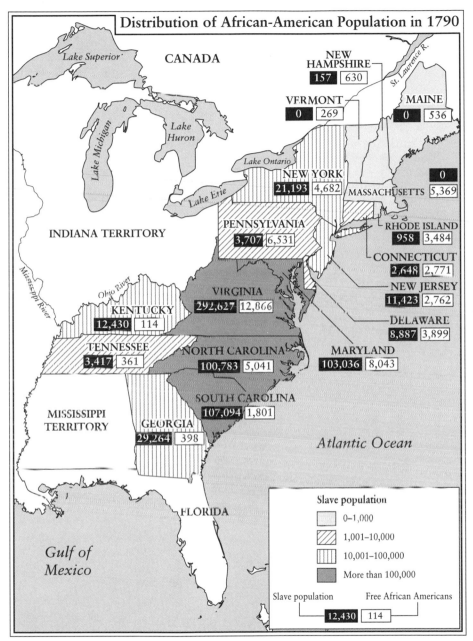

Distribution of African-American Population in 1790

CANADA

Lake Superior

Lake Michigan

Lake Huron

Lake Ontario

Lake Erie

INDIANA TERRITORY

Mississippi River

Ohio River

NEW HAMPSHIRE
157 | 630

VERMONT
0 | 269

MAINE
0 | 536

St. Lawrence R.

NEW YORK
21,193 | 4,682

MASSACHUSETTS
0 | 5,369

PENNSYLVANIA
3,707 | 6,531

RHODE ISLAND
958 | 3,484

CONNECTICUT
2,648 | 2,771

NEW JERSEY
11,423 | 2,762

VIRGINIA
292,627 | 12,866

DELAWARE
8,887 | 3,899

KENTUCKY
12,430 | 114

TENNESSEE
3,417 | 361

NORTH CAROLINA
100,783 | 5,041

MARYLAND
103,036 | 8,043

SOUTH CAROLINA
107,094 | 1,801

MISSISSIPPI TERRITORY

GEORGIA
29,264 | 398

FLORIDA

Atlantic Ocean

Gulf of Mexico

Slave population

	0–1,000
	1,001–10,000
	10,001–100,000
	More than 100,000

Slave population   Free African Americans
12,430 | 114

Shortly after creation of the United States, nearly a fifth of all Americans were black, but nine out of every ten African Americans were slaves. Although slavery was rapidly disappearing in the North, more than half of all free African Americans lived in the South in 1790.

try. In the South, where slavery expanded rapidly through this period, whites lived in fear of slave insurrections. They regarded free blacks as unwelcome examples and as potentially dangerous agitators whom they did not want around. As a consequence, conditions for free blacks in the South steadily worsened, until many were little better off than slaves.

Meanwhile, it was natural for former slaves to expect to find some semblance of freedom in the Northern states, where slavery had largely disappeared. Even there, however, the cloud of slavery in the South loomed over race relations. The growth of Southern slavery helped to harden Northern prejudices against free blacks. Many Northern whites supported abolition—for both selfless and selfish reasons—but few were prepared to welcome large numbers of former slaves into their own states. Regarding slavery as a Southern problem, Northerners wanted Southern blacks to stay where they were. As soon as it became evident that free African Americans wanted to settle in Northern and western states, legal barriers were put up to keep them out. As was the case during the colonial era, institutions of segregation did not arise amid slave societies, but within social systems containing substantial numbers of free African Americans. Thus, as more and more African Americans became free, the white impulse to restrict their freedoms grew, manifesting itself in the institutions of segregation. Had slavery ended in the South when it did in the North, the institutions of segregation might never have developed as rigidly as they did.

Among the remarkable features of the U.S. Constitution that was written in 1787—as well as the Bill of Rights that followed four years later—was its color blindness, despite its being framed in the midst of heated debates over the future of slavery. Nevertheless, aside from certain special provisions for Native Americans, the Constitution contained nothing that could be interpreted as favoring, or discriminating against, any citizens on the basis of their race, color, or creed. The Constitution held out wonderful guarantees of liberty, democracy, equal justice under law, and much more. African Americans discovered that while the government of the United States may have been founded on principles of liberty and equality, this was not necessarily true of the individual states. And it was the states—not the national government —that made and enforced most of the laws that affected day-to-day life.

For their political and legal rights, Americans had to look to the state governments, whose laws could and did vary enormously. By the time the Civil War began in 1861, there were 34 states in the Union. The governments of virtually all of them had laws discriminating against African Americans. The federal government was involved only to the extent that it approved the constitutions of new states before admitting them to the Union. Many state constitutions contained rules designed to exclude African Americans, voting laws that used racial criteria for determining who had the franchise, and other discriminatory clauses. The constitution of the state of Missouri, which was formed in 1821, provides a typical example. That document condoned slavery—which was not against federal law—but it also authorized the legislature to enact laws that would prevent African Americans from entering the state. Such exclusionary rules clearly contradicted the federal Constitution's explicit guarantee that "the citizens of each State shall be entitled to all Privileges and Immunities of Citizens in the several states" (article 4, section 2). Missouri's political leaders got Congress to approve discriminatory clauses in their new state constitution by citing precedent in the constitutions of most other states. However, the federal Constitution's "Privileges and Immunities" clause raised a more fundamental question: Could African Americans be considered citizens of the United States?

In 1857 when the U.S. Supreme Court considered the case of *Dred Scott v. Sandford*, it had a unique opportunity to resolve questions about both the future of slavery in the

If any slave hereafter emancipated, shall remain within this Commonwealth more than twelve months after his or her right to freedom shall have accrued, he or she shall forfeit all such right, and may be apprehended and sold . . .

◆

—Virginia Statute on Slaves, Free Negroes, and Mulattoes (1819)

nation and the legal status of free African Americans. Instead, the Court passed down one of the most backward-looking decisions in its history. It ruled that Congress had no power to prohibit slavery in any U.S. territory, thereby voiding the Missouri Compromise of 1820 which said that the United States had to maintain an equal number of states allowing slavery and those prohibiting it. Even worse, the Court ruled that African Americans were not, and could not be, citizens of the United States.

It would not be until after the Civil War that the federal government began intervening in the states in positive ways, by requiring them to extend citizenship and full political and legal rights to African Americans. However, the bitter legacy left by slavery and by the Civil War itself ensured that it would take another full century before the federal government could commit itself to guaranteeing equal rights to all citizens. In the meantime, African Americans would find the early years of American nationhood a grim era.

The Revolutionary War began in 1770, when British troops fired on a crowd of American colonists in Boston. Black Bostonian Crispus Attucks is now honored as a patriot because he was among the first Americans killed in what came to be known as the Boston Massacre. Afterward, fighting between British soldiers and American colonists gradually evolved from skirmishes to battles, and finally into a full-scale war. During the conflict's early years, fighting was irregular, and American forces were not fully organized. A number of free blacks, such as Lemuel Haynes of Connecticut, fought with distinction in various patriot military units.

Despite the service record of African Americans, many whites hesitated to trust their devotion. Most African Americans were slaves who stood to gain little from an American victory, unless they won freedom for themselves. Because the war was fought among English-speaking combatants—including many on both sides with local roots—it had some of the characteristics of a civil war. This situation gave African Americans—especially slaves—an unprecedented opportunity to better their own condition by supporting the side that offered them more.

When George Washington assumed command of the Continental Army in June 1775 he insisted that slaves not be allowed to serve. He feared that if disaffected slaves were armed, they might organize insurrections. Several months later a committee of the Continental Congress—whose membership included Benjamin Franklin—decided to exclude both slaves and free blacks from the Continental Army. The individual states soon followed suit by restricting service to whites in their own military units. This American readiness to exclude blacks from service was based partly on the mistaken assumption that the war would not last long.

Meanwhile, the British—who were anxious to build up their troop strength from local manpower—did not share American inhibitions about recruiting slaves. In November 1775 Lord Dunmore, the British governor of Virginia, proclaimed that all male slaves who joined the British forces would be liberated. Several days later, Washington—apparently unaware of Dunmore's proclamation—issued formal orders not to recruit African Americans into the Continental Army. He soon realized, however, that so many slaves were accepting Britain's offer of freedom that he must reverse his own position. In December he recommended accepting free blacks into his army, and he later decided to accept slaves as well. As the war progressed, the difficulty of recruiting white troops increased, and colonies began matching British offers to give slaves their freedom in return for military service.

By the time the war ended, nearly 10,000 African Americans had served in the colonial armies; about half of these fought as regular soldiers. The fact that nearly 30,000 African Americans served the British—mostly in non-combat roles—says much about who offered them better opportunities for freedom. During the peace negotiations that followed the conflict, return of fugitive slaves was a major American objective. The British, however, insisted on taking their black allies away with them; many of these former slaves then resettled in Nova Scotia and the West Indies.

The Continental Army was a new organization made up of existing colonial militias and newly drafted units. Because it evolved in response to the changing demands of the war, the conditions of service for its troops varied greatly among units. Most of the black soldiers who fought on the American side served in integrated units, but there were also a handful of segregated units. Rhode Island, for example, enlisted 100 African Americans in one battalion and scattered hundreds more among other, mostly white, units. New York and Massachusetts also fielded several all-black units. It appears, however, that few Continental Army units were entirely white. A Hessian soldier who served with the Americans wrote at the time that there was no American regiment "in which there are not Negroes in abundance, and among them are able-bodied, strong and brave fellows."

In 1779 Henry Laurens, a South Carolina merchant, got approval from Washington and the Continental Congress to recruit and train 3,000 African-American soldiers. South Carolina's own legislature killed his plan—probably out of fear of losing too many slaves. A letter that Alexander Hamilton wrote to the Continental Congress about Laurens's plan says much about the nature of racial prejudice at that time:

> I have not the least doubt that the Negroes will make very excellent soldiers, with proper management. . . . I

hear it frequently objected to the scheme of embodying Negroes that they are too stupid to make soldiers. This is so far from appearing to me a valid objection . . . for their natural faculties are as good as ours . . . The contempt we have been taught to entertain for the blacks, makes us fancy many things that are founded neither in reason nor experience; and an unwillingness to part with property of so valuable a kind, will furnish a thousand arguments to show the impracticability, or pernicious tendency of a scheme which requires such sacrifices. But it should be considered, that if we do not make use of them in this way, the enemy probably will, and that the best way to counteract the temptations they will hold out, will be to offer them ourselves. An essential part of the plan is to give them freedom with their swords. This will secure their fidelity, animate their courage, and, I believe will have a good influence upon those that remain, by opening a door to their emancipation.

About 2,000 African Americans served in American naval units during the Revolutionary War. This number was smaller than that of those who served in the army, but it represented a larger portion of the total naval manpower.

America's Revolutionary War wrested independence from Britain, but it did not settle all the issues that caused friction between Britain and America. Unresolved issues, such as Britain's impressment habit of seizing American sailors and forcing them to serve in the Royal Navy, led to a second war in 1812. It was a time when Britain was engaged in a life-and-death war with France and had limited resources to devote to its less dangerous conflict with the United States.

The number of African Americans who served in the War of 1812 was small, despite the fact that there was less opposition to recruiting them than there had been in the earlier war. The reason lay partly in the fact that most free blacks lived in the Middle Atlantic and New England states, where there was no strong support for the war. The few

African Americans who did serve in the war were scattered throughout mostly white army units. Most of them served in menial capacities, but some did have opportunities to distinguish themselves in fighting. Their most notable contributions came in the Battle of New Orleans, after Andrew Jackson made a special appeal to black recruits.

Although the new American navy had forbidden the enlistment of African Americans on U.S. warships at the end of the 18th century, African Americans played a much more significant role in the navy than in the army during the War of 1812. When Commodore William Perry captured a British squadron on Lake Erie in September 1813, at least a tenth—and possibly as many as a quarter—of the men in his Great Lakes fleet were African Americans. Before this battle, Perry had complained when African-American sailors were sent to reinforce his crews. However, Commodore Isaac Chauncey encouraged him to welcome the black sailors.

As in the Revolutionary War, many slaves went over to the British side in their quest for freedom. Others fought on the American side in the hope that they would be liberated, only to be disappointed after the war ended.

> I have yet to learn that the color of the skin . . . can affect a man's qualifications or usefulness. I have nearly 50 blacks on board this ship, and many of them are among my best men.
>
> ◆
>
> —Commodore Isaac Chauncey, letter to Captain Oliver Hazard Perry, September 1813

Despite the generally excellent service record of African Americans in the Revolutionary War and the War of 1812, South Carolina senator John C. Calhoun—a former vice president of the United States—later submitted a bill to exclude African Americans from serving in the military, except as cooks and servants. The Senate passed Calhoun's bill in 1842, but the House of Representatives—in which the South had less influence—never voted on it.

At the moment American independence was recognized in 1783,

the most striking difference between the North and South was the extent to which each region's economy depended on slavery. About 90 percent of the slaves in the country lived in the five original Southern states, by that time the Northern states were moving quickly toward abolishing slavery completely. Vermont had officially ended slavery in 1777; Pennsylvania and the rest of the New England states quickly followed. By 1830 slavery was virtually abolished in the North. Only New Jersey held on a little longer. By that time there were almost three times more slaves living in the South than there had been in the entire country at independence. After another 30 years, that number would double.

The North abolished slavery earlier than the South for one compelling reason: The institution had not taken root there as it had in the South. In contrast to the South—with its large plantation farm systems—the North's economy did not depend on slave labor. Indeed, white workers in the North actively opposed slavery—not so much for humanitarian reasons, but because they regarded slave labor as unfair competition for wage laborers. Furthermore, the numbers of slaves within the individual Northern states were not great enough to make white workers afraid of being swamped by cheaper black labor. The North was thus able to abolish slavery without endangering its economy.

While slavery still existed in both regions, another crucial difference between them was that some Northern states allowed their slaves legal rights. In Massachusetts, for example, slaves occasionally even won their freedom in court by successfully challenging their masters' right to own them. Indeed, it was a court decision—not legislative action—that ended slavery in Massachusetts in 1783. With a victory such as that as a precedent, black Massachusetts residents naturally regarded the courts as their allies in later efforts to gain their full rights. As early as the 1840s, African Americans in Massachusetts won school desegregation cases in the courts a century before the National Association for the Advancement of Colored People (NAACP) tried the same strategy.

After the Treaty of Paris recognized the independence of the American colonies in 1783, the new nation attempted to govern itself with the Articles of Confederation that had carried it through the Revolutionary War. Soon it became clear, however, that a much stronger central government was necessary, and representatives of the 13 original states met in Philadelphia in 1787 to frame the new constitution that has been the law of the land ever since.

When the framers of the Constitution met, abolition of slavery was a major issue separating representatives of the Northern and Southern states. However, the framers did manage to agree *not* to abolish the importation of slaves into the United States before 1808. By the time that year arrived, most of the Northern states had abolished slavery completely within their borders. The Southern states might have followed suit, but something happened after the ratification of the Constitution that gave slavery a new impulse to grow.

In 1793 Eli Whitney, a New Englander living in Georgia, invented a ginning machine that dramatically improved the efficiency of cotton farming by reducing the amount of human labor needed to separate cotton seeds from cotton fiber. The invention appeared at a moment when the Industrial Revolution's advances in cloth manufacturing were raising world demand for cotton to new levels. The combination of expanded opportunities to sell cotton and the ability to produce it more cheaply revived the South's cotton industry, which had been on the brink of collapse. Ironically, the labor-saving advancement that saved the industry also saved slavery from extinction. While the cotton gin made cotton-fiber processing much more efficient, abundant cheap labor was still needed to raise and harvest cotton. The South supplied that labor by increasing the numbers of its slaves.

As the new Constitution had authorized, Congress outlawed importing slaves in 1808. However, the new federal law was never effectively enforced; moreover, Southern plantations deliberately sought to increase the slave population already resident through reproduction. As a consequence, the number of slaves in the United States rose from about 1 million in 1808 to around 4 million in 1860. Thus, by the time the Civil War started, the number of slaves in the United States was greater than the total population of the country had been at the time of independence. Meanwhile, Congress passed the Missouri Compromise in 1820 in order to maintain a balance between free and slave states in the Union, while prohibiting slavery in the western regions of the vast territory known as the Louisiana Purchase.

One dramatic change in black-white relations after independence was the rapid development of segregation in Christian churches. Under slavery, it was common for black slaves to attend church services with their masters' families. The churches played a leading role in the abolitionist movement;

In the early 19th century, black churches became important to African Americans as community centers and sanctuaries from white control. (Courtesy Library of Congress, Prints and Photographs Division)

Segregation in the Churches _____

In 1787—the year in which the U.S. Constitution was framed—Richard Allen and Absalom Jones walked out of a white church in Philadelphia after they were not allowed to pray. Later, they formed the first major black American church, the African Methodist Episcopal Church, with Allen as its first bishop. Allen recalled their experience:

> A number of us usually attended St. George's church in Fourth street; and when the colored people began to get numerous in attending the church, they moved us from the seats we usually sat on, and placed us around the wall, and on Sabbath morning we went to church and the sexton stood at the door, and told us to go in the gallery. He told us to go, and we would see where to sit. We expected to take the seats over the ones we formerly occupied below, not knowing any better. We took those seats. Meeting had begun, and they were nearly done singing, and just as we got to the seats, the elder said, "Let us pray." We had not been long upon our knees

afterward they might have taken the logical next step, of fully integrating African Americans into their own memberships, but this did not happen.

The separation of the American colonies from Britain also caused the separation of American Protestant denominations from their mother churches in England. The resulting reorganization of the American churches was a major distraction that diverted the attention of the churches away from the question of what to do about African-American members. Meanwhile, as African Americans in the North became free, they found themselves unwelcome in most churches that were run by whites. Some churches would not admit them at all; others would grudgingly allow them inside, then usher them to separate seating sections.

Among all the activities in which African Americans had to endure segregation, attending segregated churches was before I heard considerable scuffling and low talking. I raised my head up and saw one of the trustees, H—— M—— having hold of the Rev. Absalom Jones, pulling him up off of his knees, and saying, "You must get up —— must not kneel here." Mr. Jones replied, "Wait until prayer is over." Mr. H—— M—— said "No, you must get up now, or I will call for aid and force you away." Mr. Jones said, "Wait until prayer is over, and I well get up and trouble you no more." With that he beckoned to one of the other trustees, Mr. L—— S—— to come to his assistance. He came, and went to William White to pull him up. By this time prayer was over, and we all went out of the church in a body, and they were no more plagued with us in the church. This raised a great excitement and inquiry among the citizens, so much that I believe they were ashamed of their conduct. But my dear Lord was with us, and we were filled with fresh vigor to get a house erected to worship God in. Seeing our forlorn and distressed situation, many of the hearts of our citizens were moved to urge us forward; notwithstanding we had subscribed largely towards finishing St. George's church, in building the gallery and laying new floors, and just as the house was made comfortable, we were turned out from enjoying the comforts of worshipping therein. We then hired a store-room, and held worship by ourselves. . . .◆

perhaps the least tolerable. Religion became the area in which African Americans worked the hardest to assert their own independence, and they wasted little time in forming their own churches. In 1787 Richard Allen and Absalom Jones had organized a branch Episcopal church for African Americans after they were treated rudely in a Philadelphia church. From this beginning grew the African Methodist Episcopal Church (AMEC). AMEC branches arose in other towns in the North and in the mid-Atlantic slave states that had large free black populations. Eventually, the AMEC became one of the largest blacks churches in the United States.

The African Methodist Episcopal Zion Church had a similar beginning a decade later, after African Americans withdrew from a Methodist Episcopal church in New York City. In 1809 black Baptists in Philadelphia and Boston formed their own churches for the same reasons. After the

Reverend Thomas Paul helped form Boston's first black Baptist church, he also helped form the famous Abyssinian Baptist Church in New York City. As the century progressed, the Baptist churches attracted more black members than other denominations.

Independent black churches proved to be important training grounds for leadership within black communities, and the churches themselves assumed even stronger roles within the black communities than they did within white communities. A typical leader was John Melvin, who had been born free in Virginia. After moving to Cleveland, Ohio, he did well operating a cargo vessel on Lake Michigan. Eventually, he helped organize a Baptist church, in which he insisted on nonsegregated seating, and he later helped organize Cleveland's first school for African-American children. During the early years of independence, African Americans were also quick to form fraternal and mutual aid societies to help each other out. In Boston, for example, 44 African Americans joined together to form the African Society in 1796.

NOTES

p. 42 "in which there are not Negroes . . ." Quoted in Peter M. Bergman, *Chronological History of the Negro* (New York: NAL, 1969), p. 55.

pp. 42–43 "I have not the least doubt . . ." Quoted in Bergman, *Chronological History of the Negro*, p. 57.

p. 44 "I have yet to learn . . ." Quoted in Bergman, *Chronological History of the Negro*, p. 98.

pp. 48–49 "A number of us . . ." Quoted in Leslie H. Fishel, Jr., and Benjamin Quarles, eds., *The Negro American: A Documentary History* (New York: Scott, Foresman and Co., 1967), pp. 141–42.

4

Slavery for the South, Segregation for the North

Although Congress had outlawed the slave trade in 1808, the institution of slavery was stronger than ever a dozen years later, and it was becoming a divisive issue for the nation. Politicians in both the North and the South were concerned about maintaining an approximate balance between free and slave states. The vast increase in territory that the Louisiana Purchase brought to the United States in 1803 ensured that many more states would be created. By 1819 nine new states had already joined the original 13, and Maine and Missouri were about to apply for admission. In order to maintain the balance, Congress passed legislation known as the Missouri Compromise. Until the Supreme Court ruled it unconstitutional in 1857, that agreement helped to keep the numbers of free and slave states nearly equal.

As the North and South grew further apart, the two regions developed quite different patterns of race relations. Meanwhile, African Americans still living under slavery did not simply accept their lot quietly. During the four decades preceding the Civil War, there were more and larger slave revolts than ever before, and the numbers of runaway slaves increased greatly. Meanwhile, Northern African Americans played leading roles in the abolitionist movement and in the Underground Railroad, a loosely organized network that helped runaway slaves to escape to the North.

Racial segregation has come to be regarded as an essentially Southern phenomenon. There are reasons for this belief. During the 20th century, the South would be the region to develop the institutions of racial segregation most fully. However, the South actually copied many of its discriminatory practices from institutions that had been developed in the North during the early 19th century. The irony is that the main institutions of segregation arose not in slave states but in free states. After slavery was abolished in the Northern states, white Northerners were initially inclined to be tolerant toward free African Americans. However, as slavery expanded in the South and growing numbers of blacks migrated north, whites came to regard them as a threat, and they responded with new laws and customs to control them.

Newly freed African Americans quickly discovered that being legally free did not in itself automatically improve their condition. Landless, poor, and uneducated, former slaves found that they were still regarded as members of a despised race. In 1790 Boston clergyman Jeremy Belknap had observed that many former slaves in Massachusetts were much worse off than they had been under slavery. Their distinctive appearance, their former servitude, and their impoverished condition all contributed to their being badly treated by whites. Unable to merge easily into the dominant white communities that surrounded them, they remained highly visible and unwelcome minorities in most Northern cities. As their numbers grew, white prejudice against them increased. With this increasing prejudice came new forms of discrimination and segregation.

After the French aristocrat Alexis de Tocqueville traveled through the United States during the early 1830s, he wrote *Democracy in America*. Among his observations is the comment that race prejudice "appears to be stronger in the states that have abolished slavery than in those where it still exists; and nowhere is it so intolerant as in those states where servitude has never been known." Despite the poor economic conditions in which most Northern African Americans lived, however, there was no letup in migration to the North. No matter how hard conditions became, former slaves never showed any signs of wishing to return to slavery or the South.

A striking manifestation of the Northern states' fears of African Americans was their passage of laws designed to keep them out altogether. Northerners advanced a number of questionable arguments to justify keeping African Americans in the South. For example, some people argued that as descendants of tropical Africans, black people could not thrive in the colder climates of the Northern United States.

In 1821 the state legislature of Massachusetts appointed a committee to investigate restricting the immigration of free blacks. White residents of Philadelphia—located only the width of the Delaware River away from slave territory—campaigned to stop the flow of free blacks and fugitive slaves into their city.

Apart from slavery, the gravest form of discrimination that African Americans endured almost everywhere was denial of full political and legal rights. Disfranchisement and exclusion from the courts were forms of segregation in themselves; they also handicapped African-American efforts to combat other forms of segregation—in schools, public accommodations, transportation, housing, and elsewhere. An example of the crucial importance of political rights can be seen in what occurred in Ohio in 1839, when African Americans petitioned the state legislature to repeal its laws against African-American immigration. The legislature dismissed the petition by declaring that blacks residents had no constitutional right to petition it for any purpose. For reasons such as this, African Americans made attainment of their full civil rights and liberties a primary goal.

Nothing in the original U.S. Constitution guaranteed or denied the vote to anyone. Until the post–Civil War years, individual states had sole authority to award the franchise, or right to vote. Some states traditionally excluded blacks from voting as early as colonial times. In 1705, for example, Virginia enacted a law forbidding African Americans and American Indians from holding public offices or testifying in court. In 1723 the colony explicitly denied free blacks the right to vote.

State constitutions written during the Revolutionary era generally did not exclude African Americans from voting, but this condition did not endure. After 1789 every new Southern state admitted to the Union except Tennessee took the vote away from African Americans, and Tennessee followed in 1834. Around the turn of the century there had been a general movement to disfranchise blacks. In 1802 President Thomas Jefferson himself signed a bill taking away the vote of black residents of the District of Columbia—the only part of the country in which the federal government determined franchise qualifications. Individual states in both the North and the South followed this example. By 1830 few African Americans were voting anywhere in the United States.

Few states permitted blacks to serve on juries or to testify against whites in court. This meant that in legal disputes with white parties, African Americans could expect to lose. However, African Americans were not completely without legal rights, at least in some Northern states. They could, and often

As the century progressed, restrictions on free blacks grew progressively stricter—especially during periods when slaves made trouble for their masters. South Carolina, for example, had an 1820 statute requiring the imprisonment onshore of all black sailors on ships entering its ports. Using the federal Constitution's commerce clause to invalidate this state legislation, a Supreme Court justice doing circuit court duty in the region ruled the South Carolina law unconstitutional (his decision would have important broader implications). In his ruling, Associate Justice William Johnson articulated some important questions about where the lines of segregation were to be drawn:

> The object of this law, and it has been so acknowledged in argument, is to prohibit ships coming into this port employing colored seamen, whether citizens or subject of their government or not. But if this state can prohibit Great Britain from employing her colored subjects . . . or if at liberty to prohibit the employment of her subjects of the African race, why not prohibit her from using those of Irish or of Scottish nativity? If the color of his skin is to preclude the Lascar or the Sierra Leone seaman, why not the color of his eye or his hair exclude from our ports the inhabitants of her other territories?

Delaware, though a border state, was typical among slave states in passing a law in 1852 barring free blacks from outside the state from obtaining legal residence. The law further stipulated that any black resident who left Delaware for a period longer than 60 days could not return. The laws also barred blacks from voting or holding public office.

It has been said that the condition of free blacks in the South deteriorated so much by the time of the Civil War that there was little real difference between them and slaves. This might be an exaggeration; however, it is significant that most of the Southern states enacted laws during the 1850s that offered free blacks the chance to choose their own masters and re-enslave themselves. In 1859, Arkansas even passed a law that threatened to re-enslave all the free blacks who remained in the state by the end of the year. In such a climate, it was no wonder that thousands of African Americans moved to the North.

The geographical distribution of people in the United States has shifted continuously since the colonial era, and its rate of change has been accelerated by certain events. The U.S. purchase of the Louisiana Territory from France in 1803 was one such event. The sudden doubling of the size of the United States encouraged people to move west to open the new lands. During this same period, the abolition of slavery in the North gave tens of thousands of African Americans a choice about where to live for the first time, and many of them joined the westward movement. Meanwhile, many free blacks from the Southern slave states went north in search of opportunities to enjoy their freedom. The result was rapid increases in the black populations of both Northern states and western territories.

During the 1850s alone, the black populations of midwestern and western states tripled. Many white residents of these states resented the influx of blacks, particularly the recent arrivals from the South. In addition to using legislation to discourage African Americans from migrating to these regions, whites occasionally simply drove them away. White violence against blacks was especially strong in areas bordering the slave states, such as southern Ohio. In 1829, for example, whites drove about 1,000 African Americans out of Cincinnati. The following year another mob of white Ohioans drove eight African Americans out of Portsmouth, another town on the Ohio River. Additional white violence against African Americans erupted during the 1830s in other Northern cities, including New York City and Philadelphia.

Among the most visible manifestations of segregation in the North were in housing and public accommodations.

Most major cities limited where African Americans could live and had well-defined black neighborhoods. Boston, for example, had areas known as "Nigger Hill" and "Little Guinea." Cincinnati had a "Little Africa." Similar neighborhoods could be found in Philadelphia, New York City, and elsewhere.

Southern cities tended not to have black ghettoes. Most black Southerners were slaves whose conditions of bondage made segregation unnecessary, as had been the case during the colonial era. Except in North Carolina, most Southern free blacks lived in the cities and did not have to deal with severe forms of institutionalized segregation until after the Reconstruction era, following the Civil War.

Only a river's width distant from slave territory, Cincinnati naturally attracted African Americans fleeing the South before the Civil War. With whites going to great lengths to make them feel unwelcome, the city's African Americans had special reason to seek solace in their churches. (Courtesy Library of Congress, Prints and Photographs Division)

Although social and political conditions for free blacks were generally harsher in the Southern states than in the North—where all African Americans were legally free—the South offered them better job opportunities, particularly in the mechanical trades. Most trade unions in both regions barred African Americans from membership. In the Northern states skilled black laborers had to compete more directly than in the South with white workers, who continued to pour into the country from Europe.

Emancipation gave free African Americans greater opportunities for traveling and using their time as they wished than they had enjoyed while slavery existed. The early 19th century was the first era in which large numbers of African Americans moved about without the supervision of white masters. However, this also resulted in an increase in segregated arrangements in travel conveyances and public inns and eating establishments. When slaves had traveled with their masters, they could go wherever their masters went and they were subject to the conditions imposed on servants; racial segregation was largely irrelevant. Free African Americans, however, often found traveling more difficult as operators of various forms of public transportation began refusing them services.

In 1838 African Americans in Massachusetts found segregation on trains, stagecoaches, and steamboats intolerable and petitioned the legislature to end it. Although the legislature did not act on their petition, segregation did gradually disappear from trains in Massachusetts.

The United States has never had anything like a national educational system. During the early days of independence, American education was largely a local matter, with most schools run by churches or private teachers. However, this period was characterized by a widespread movement to establish and improve schools. Eventually, education came to be seen as a responsibility of the states, which started funding and supervising schools operated by municipalities.

In slave-holding states whites generally were strongly opposed to educating African-American slaves. This attitude also carried over to free blacks; some Southern states even outlawed teaching free blacks—probably out of fear that they would study ideas that would encourage them to rebel against the social order. Restrictions on African-American education could be quite rigid. For example, in 1838 African Americans in Fredericksburg, Virginia, petitioned the state legislature for permission to send their children out of the state for education, but even that simple request was denied.

In nonslave states there was some white sentiment in favor of educating free blacks. Practices varied from city to city. Early government-run schools in Rochester, New York, for example, were integrated, but those in New York City were not. By mid-century, Ohio had racially segregated public schools, but Illinois and Indiana had no public schools at all for African Americans. Patterns varied from state to state, and not always as one might expect. For example, the New England states were generally more accommodating to African Americans than other parts of the country, but they also could behave in surprisingly racist manners. In 1832 a white teacher named Prudence Crandall admitted a black girl to her private school in Canterbury, Connecticut. The townspeople protested strongly, and some white students withdrew from Crandall's school. Nevertheless, she admitted more black students, until the state legislature enacted a law forbidding out-of-state African Americans from attending Connecticut schools without local permission. Eventually

W*ith reference to the wrongs inflicted and injures received on railroads by persons of color, I need not say they do not end with the termination of the route, but, in effect, tend to discourage, disparage and depress this class of citizens.*

◆

—Charles Lenox Remond, speech to committee of Massachusetts House of Representatives, February 1842

Crandall was jailed and her school was demolished by white vandals.

African Americans did speak out against segregated education. In 1837 the weekly magazine *The Colored American* denounced segregated schools because they "so shackled the intellect of colored youth." Recognizing the value of education, African Americans did not wait for the generosity of whites to provide schools. Instead, they organized schools for their own children, often with the help of their churches. African Americans everywhere were anxious for education, but nowhere were they better organized and more assertive than in Boston. That city established an African-American school in 1820, but it scarcely met the needs of the black community, which was scattered through the city. Through the 1840s black Bostonians persistently demanded access to the city's white schools by petitioning the government and taking legal action.

In 1849 Benjamin F. Roberts sued Boston for not allowing his daughter to attend white public schools. Arguing a case remarkably similar to those that would be fought by the NAACP a century later, attorneys Charles Sumner and Robert Morris cited the clause of the Massachusetts state constitution stating that "all men, without distinction of color or race, are equal before the law." They carried Roberts's case all the way to the U.S. Supreme Court. Unfortunately, the Court validated segregated schools, thereby setting a precedent for the separate but equal doctrine that would later become a byword for segregation. However, although Roberts lost his case, the Massachusetts legislature amended the state's school laws in 1855, so that "In determining the qualifications of scholars to be admitted into any public school or any district school in the Commonwealth, no distinction shall be made on account of the race, color or religious opinions, of the applicant or scholar."

It was even more difficult for African Americans to enter institutions of higher learning. Out of the estimated 4 million

African Americans in the United States on the eve of the Civil War, only 28 are known to have received college degrees by that time. The first African Americans to earn degrees got them at Amherst and Bowdoin in 1826; however, Ohio's Oberlin College was the first college to formally welcome African Americans in 1834.

The limited opportunities that African Americans had for higher education moved philanthropic whites to organize all-black colleges. Finding suitable locations for such institutions was not always easy. In 1831, for example, whites in New Haven, Connecticut, voted overwhelmingly to keep a proposed black college out of their city. The first all-black college to open was the Institute for Colored Youth (later renamed Cheyney State University) in Cheyney, Pennsylvania, in 1837. Ashmun Institute (renamed Lincoln University after the Civil War) opened in 1854 in Oxford, Pennsylvania. Ohio's Wilberforce University followed in 1856. Established and run by white philanthropists, these early colleges stressed practical training and religious education in their curricula. After the Civil War hundreds more such colleges were created to meet the needs of freed slaves.

Closely related to efforts to exclude black immigrants from many states were proposals to remove African Americans completely from North America. By mid-century, even Abraham Lincoln would be among the supporters of "colonization" as a solution to the question of what to do with African Americans. As with exclusionary movements, white interest in colonization schemes grew apace with the rising prospects of total abolition of slavery.

Proposals to send blacks back to Africa had been expressed at least as early as 1714. In 1777 Thomas Jefferson headed a committee in Virginia's state legislature that developed a gradual emancipation plan for slaves that would lead to their being sent to Africa. Motives behind colonization schemes were mixed. Many white advocates of colonization had a sincere humanitarian desire to see African Americans prosper. They favored extending full political and social equality to blacks, but believed that because this would never come about, African Americans would be better off going elsewhere. Other whites supported colonization out of selfish and often racist impulses to rid America of black people, whom they regarded as incapable of adapting to "civilized" society. Many slave owners hoped that deporting free blacks would help ensure the perpetuation of slavery in the United States. Finally, many whites thought that African Americans could carry Christianity and Western civilization to what they regarded as a benighted (unenlightened) land because it lacked the Gospel.

The biggest of the colonization schemes began in 1816, when the American Colonization Society was formed to resettle freed slaves in Africa. This organization received support from the majority of state legislatures and such prominent figures as Henry Clay and Francis Scott Key, and it received a $100,000 donation from the U.S. Congress.

Overall, the impact of colonization movements on African Americans was negligible. Over three decades, the American Colonization Society and similar organizations settled less than 15,000 African Americans in West Africa. This figure represented less than one half of one percent of the black people then in the United States. Most of the African Americans who were sent to Africa came from slave states. Northern blacks were solidly opposed to colonization, as were many white abolitionists—who were suspicious of the support that Southern slave owners gave to such schemes. Despite the discrimination that free African Americans faced, they were not anxious to leave the United States to face the uncertain hardships of Africa, particularly without sufficient funds and supplies to ensure success. Nonetheless, enough African Americans emigrated to West Africa to found the independent nation of Liberia in 1847.

The rationale behind colonization schemes rested on two central points: First, that African Americans as a people were too degraded to have hope of ever fitting into American society. Second, that African Americans could perform a service to humanity by "returning" to Africa and helping to uplift the "backward" people of that benighted land. One outspoken African-American opponent of colonization was Peter Williams, the pastor of a New York Episcopal church. Williams recognized the contradiction in the arguments advanced for colonization schemes. If black people are too degraded to find a place in America, he asked, what sense does it make to send them to Africa? He said, "If we are as vile and degraded as they represent us, and they wish the Africans to be rendered a virtuous, enlightened and happy people, they should not *think* of sending *us* among them, lest we should make them worse instead of better." Williams went on to explain what African Americans really wanted:

> We are *natives* of this country, we ask only to be treated as well as *foreigners*. Not a few of our fathers suffered and bled to purchase its independence; we ask only to be treated as well as those who fought against it. We have toiled to cultivate it, and raise it to its present prosperous condition; we ask only to share equal privileges with those who come from distant lands, to enjoy the fruits of our labour. Let these moderate requests be granted, and we need not go to Africa or anywhere else to be improved and happy . . .

Williams went on to complain that the well-intentioned work of the colonization society was making things even worse for free blacks by misrepresenting their moral character and behavior in order to advance the case for sending African Americans out of the country. One result of this negative publicity was increasing restrictions on the movement of free blacks among the states. Finally, Williams said that while the colonization society claimed to have no intention of sending African Americans to Africa without their consent, it was contributing so much to making it intolerable for them to live in the United States that if "no other door is open to receive us but Africa, our removal there will be anything but voluntary."

NOTES

p. 53   "appears to be stronger . . ." Quoted in C. Vann Woodward, *The Strange Career of Jim Crow* (2d ed., New York: Oxford University Press, 1966), p. 20.

p. 56   "*Be it therefore enacted*, . . ." Quoted in Albert P. Blaustein and Robert L. Zangrando, *Civil Rights and the Black American: A Documentary History* (New York: Clarion Books, 1970), pp. 64–65.

p. 56   "a free negro . . ." Quoted in Blaustein and Zangrando, *Civil Rights and the Black American: A Documentary History,* p. 68.

p. 57   "The object of this law, . . ." Quoted in Blaustein and Zangrando, *Civil Rights and the Black American: A Documentary History,* p. 87

p. 62   "all men, without distinction . . ." Quoted in Blaustein and Zangrando, *Civil Rights and the Black American: A Documentary History,* p. 122.

p. 65   "If we are as vile . . ." Quoted in Fishel and Quarles, *The Negro American: A Documentary History,* pp. 145–47.

5

Civil War and Emancipation

The failure of the new nation to resolve the problem of slavery had disastrous consequences—and not merely for the millions of people whose enslavement was prolonged. Division of the nation into slave and free states guaranteed that friction would continue between the North and the South. Many issues divided the two regions, but most of them were aggravated by the fundamental difference over slavery. Eventually the Southern states expressed their dissatisfaction with the Union by beginning to secede in late 1860. The following February—before Abraham Lincoln was even inaugurated as president—representatives of the secessionist states met to form a provisional government of their own. What followed was almost inevitable. Lincoln's new administration insisted on preserving the Union, so the two halves of the nation went to war.

Although the Civil War lasted only four years, it brought greater changes to the condition of African Americans than any other single event in U.S. history. Hundreds of thousands of African Americans served in the war. Shortly after it ended, new amendments to the Constitution abolished slavery once and for all and established beyond a doubt that African Americans were citizens of the United States. In the general political confusion that accompanied the end of the war, Southern whites tried to impose new forms of servitude on their former slaves by enacting harsh laws similar to their old slave codes. However, Northern Republicans in Congress soon took control of federal policy in the defeated South and began implementing a new order known as Reconstruction.

When the Civil War began, the North's major goal was restoring the Union. Although slavery was an important factor in the war between the states, the Civil War was not initially viewed as a crusade to abolish slavery. And no one—least of all President Lincoln—saw the war as a campaign to bring about racial equality in the United States. Indeed, in the years leading up to the war, Lincoln himself had repeatedly expressed his lack of support for racial equality. In a speech given in 1858 he said that

My *paramount object is to save the Union, and not either to save or destroy slavery. If I could save the Union without freeing any slave, I would do it; if I could save it by freeing all the slaves, I would do it; and if I could save it by freeing some and leaving others along, I would also do that.*

◆

—President Abraham Lincoln, letter to Horace Greeley, August 22, 1862

. . . there is a physical difference between the black and white races which I believe will for ever forbid the two races living together on terms of social and political equality. And inasmuch as they cannot so live, while they do remain together there must be the position of superior and inferior, and I as much as any other man am in favor of having the superior position assigned to the white race.

When the Civil War began, some Americans believed that the war itself would bring about the end of slavery. Nothing happened, however, to confirm this idea, and it was gradually abandoned. In its place, the idea of transforming the war into

Born a slave in Maryland around 1817, Frederick Douglass escaped to the North when he was 19, and he later became a newspaper publisher and abolitionist leader. During the Civil War he helped persuade President Lincoln to accept African-American volunteers in the army and then worked to recruit them himself. (Courtesy Library of Congress, Prints and Photographs Division)

a moral crusade against slavery evolved slowly. This change in thinking had much to do with military developments in the war itself. For Northerners to accept complete abolition of slavery as a goal of the war, they had to be convinced of two things: first, that once the South's millions of slaves were free, they would not pour into the North; and second, that emancipation itself would help the Union's military effort.

African Americans themselves played a leading role in transforming the war into a campaign against slavery. Through public meetings and newspapers, black leaders consistently and forcefully spoke out on this issue, echoing the sentiments expressed in Frederick Douglass's words: "Henceforth let the war cry be down with treason, and down with slavery, the cause of treason."

In late 1861 Republicans in Congress began mounting a campaign against slavery. They appealed for support, not on the basis of humanitarianism, but on the basis of patriotism. Emancipation, they argued, would help win the war by disrupting the South and freeing slaves who would then serve the Union. Meanwhile, President Lincoln contributed to preparing the North for emancipation by stressing the purely military need for it. He also had to be ready with solutions to the many problems that would arise as large numbers of slaves suddenly became free. In late September 1862 Lincoln issued a preliminary proclamation of emancipation, which effectively transformed the war into a humanitarian crusade. Northerners supported emancipation when they realized that it was essential to military success and that the solution to the problem of what would become of freed slaves would be to keep them in the South. On January 1, 1863, Lincoln issued his formal Emancipation Proclamation. This proclamation actually freed no one immediately, but it did establish the principle that all slaves in the rebel states were to become free as quickly as Union forces occupied the states.

By the middle of 1863 the campaign for emancipation was gaining support throughout the North. Fears of a black influx were subsiding, and reports were coming in of the good work that freed slaves were doing in running abandoned plantations in the South. By the following year humanitarian arguments for ending slavery were being advanced, and the campaign for emancipation was becoming a moral cause.

African Americans clamored to serve the Union forces almost as soon as the Civil War began. As early as May 1861 a handful of fugitive slaves offered their services at a fort held by the Union in Virginia. After General Benjamin F. Butler put them to work as laborers, thousands more slaves fled their Southern masters and volunteered to serve the Union. Seventy-five percent of the African Americans who eventually served in Union forces were slaves at the start of the war. Meanwhile, some Southern blacks joined the Confederate army—probably in the hope of bettering their condition if the Confederacy lasted. However, none of them ever actually saw combat for the South. Free blacks in New Orleans, for example, formed a unit called the "Native Guards," which the Confederate governor recognized as part of the Louisiana state militia. Before the war ended, however, they switched their allegiance to the Union.

In the North, despite the eagerness of free African Americans to fight for the Union, they were not officially permitted to enlist as soldiers during the first 18 months of the war. Some individual Union officers tried to form black units, but the government always stopped them; however, some individual blacks did see some army service early in the war.

The Union Navy's policy toward African Americans was strikingly different from that of the army. The navy began enlisting blacks almost immediately after the war started, and it treated them well enough to ensure that they would reenlist. The navy gave African Americans more opportunities for promotion than the army later would, and it did not practice segregation aboard ships. Maintaining racially segregated quarters would have been impractical because there was not enough space to maintain separate areas for sleeping, eating, and other activities aboard warships. As a consequence, black and white sailors ate together, bunked together, and worked together closely. About 29,000 African Americans eventually enlisted in the Union Navy. They suffered about a quarter of the navy's total battle casualties, and four of them won the navy's highest service award—the Navy Medal of Honor.

White resistance to enlisting blacks into army service arose from many of the same prejudices that fostered racial segregation generally. Some Northern Democrats complained, for example, that having white troops serve alongside black troops would force them into "unnatural and repulsive associations." Behind such assertions was the deeper fear that incorporating African Americans into the services would be the first step toward forcing racial equality throughout American society. There was a pervasive white fear—particularly in the Midwest—of what might happen if African Americans were allowed to improve their position in society. Ohio congressman Chilton A. White expressed the anxieties of many Democrats:

> The question is one of political and social equality with the negro everywhere. If you make him the instrument by which your battles are fought, the means by which your victories are won, you must treat him as a victor is entitled to be treated, with all decent and becoming respect.

The sentiment that White expressed was based on an accurate perception. Each time that African Americans have contributed to winning a war for the United States, they have afterward asked for their full share of rights—no more and no less than every segment of American society has expected for itself.

Many arguments were advanced to keep African Americans out of uniform. Despite the excellent combat records of African Americans in earlier wars, many whites believed that blacks lacked the qualities needed to fight. Coupled with that prejudice was the attitude that permitting blacks to enlist would be a tacit admission of the inadequacy of white soldiers. Gradually, however, resistance to recruiting African Americans into the army lessened. This change was due in part to the steady pressure applied by black leaders such as Frederick Douglass. It was also due to the combat deeds of individual African Americans who were already serving the Union Army unofficially, and to the steady, fine performances of the many African Americans serving in the navy.

In July 1862 Congress finally authorized the president to "employ" African Americans in the armed forces. Lincoln then proclaimed that blacks could be recruited as laborers, but he still hesitated to enlist them as combat soldiers. One of the first segregated black units to be formed was the famous 54th Massachusetts Regiment, comprising mostly free blacks, commanded by white officers. It would be another year, however, before this and other black units saw significant combat action.

Meanwhile, the war was lasting longer than many people had expected, and it was taking a heavy toll on Union ranks. As the Union lost men faster than it could replace them, white resistance to enlisting black troops continued to break down. In December 1862 Secretary of War Edwin M. Stanton proposed stationing black troops in unhealthy regions and having them raise crops to help feed the army. In January President Lincoln formally issued the Emancipation Proclamation, which included a provision for accepting freed slaves into the armed services. By spring 1863, the Union government was actively recruiting African Americans. Adjutant General Lorenzo Thomas made a particularly strong effort to recruit black soldiers in the Mississippi Valley. In May the army created the Bureau of Colored Troops to coordinate the segregated units.

By the time that the war ended, nearly 180,000 African Americans had enlisted—a figure representing more than 10 percent of the entire Union Army. A quarter of these men were free at the start of the war; the rest had been slaves who freed themselves. Although women were not formally enlisted in the army, many black women served as nurses to Union troops. Their number included abolitionist leaders Harriet Tubman and Sojourner Truth.

Once recruitment of black soldiers became Union policy, the government looked for inducements to attract recruits. One major attraction was the opportunity for education. Many individual black regiments even had their own school houses.

Despite its desperate need for soldiers, the Union Army discriminated against its new black recruits in many ways. Black soldiers typically received lower pay than their white counterparts did; they had to sign up for longer periods of enlistment; they were issued inferior firearms and other equipment; they were given the least desirable duties; and they had severely limited opportunities for promotion. Furthermore, black soldiers served with the additional burden of knowing that if they were captured by the Confederacy they might be summarily killed or returned to slavery. Indeed, one of the most shameful incidents of the entire Civil War occurred at Fort Pillow, Tennessee, in April 1864, when Confederate troops captured a Union fort and slaughtered nearly 300 black soldiers who were stationed there.

Gradually, the Union Army occupied Confederate territory, and many Southern blacks assisted in a variety of ways. Some helped captured Union soldiers escape back to their own troops; others served as spies and scouts—whose service was particularly valuable because of their familiarity with the country.

The combat record of African Americans in the Civil War was exceptional. From their first opportunities to fight, they proved themselves as brave as any troops on either side of the war. One of the first black units to win widespread recognition for its valor was the 54th Massachusetts Regiment, which led the Union assault on South Carolina's Fort Wagner in July 1863. Near the end of the war, Secretary of War Stanton reported that black troops "have proved themselves among the bravest of the brave, performing deeds of daring and shedding their blood with a heroism unsurpassed by soldiers of any other race." Often in the thick of heavy fighting, African-American troops saw more than a third of their number die in action.

After the Union garrison defending Fort Pillow, Tennessee, surrendered on April 12, 1864, the victorious Confederate troops massacred the fort's African-American defenders. The fact that serving the North threatened blacks with perils not faced by white troops rarely deterred them from fighting for the Union. (Arkent Archive)

Blacks in the Union Army _____

As more and more former slaves entered the Union Army, Northern officers came to realize that these men expected to be treated respectfully. Thomas Wentworth Higginson, a former Unitarian minister who commanded the first all-black Union regiment, wrote:

> Inexperienced officers often assumed that, because these men had been slaves before enlistment, they would bear to be treated as such afterwards. Experience proved the contrary. The more strongly we marked the difference between the slave and the soldier, the better for the regiment. . . . There were no regiments in which it was so important to observe the courtesies and proprieties of military life as in these.◆

The wartime performance of African Americans disproved earlier arguments that they could not fight. After blacks proved their worth on the battlefield, whites had to find new reasons for denying them their rights. Many whites switched from opposing black recruitment to actively supporting it. To the cynically inclined, every black soldier killed meant one less white man killed. Soon many white Americans were gleefully singing a new song, "Sambo's Right to Be Kilt."

During the two decades leading up to the Civil War, the combined numbers of freed and runaway slaves who went north averaged less than 4,000 a year. But, as with earlier wars, the number of slaves who took advantage of wartime disruptions to escape to freedom rose during the Civil War. The difficulties of surviving in the South soon forced most of the new fugitives to flee north. Tens of thousands of escaped slaves went north during the war, but the Northern press so exaggerated their numbers that a backlash against African Americans rapidly developed.

Northern opposition to black immigration arose from the same white fears that had given rise to segregation. Throughout American history, whenever large numbers of blacks tried to enter predominantly white areas, white racism grew stronger and expressed itself in calls for discriminatory legislation. During the Civil War, resistance to black immigration remained particularly strong in the Midwest, whose population was less than one percent black at the start of the war. A clear example of white fear of blacks is what occurred in Ohio in late 1861 and early 1862, when more than 30,000 citizens petitioned the state legislature to forbid further black immigration.

Transformation of the Civil War into a crusade against slavery initially had the effect of magnifying white fears of an influx of former slaves from the South. Immediately after the Emancipation Proclamation, for example, alarmed Democrats in Indiana pushed for a more stringent exclusionary law that would make illegal entry by blacks into Indiana a felony offense. As the war progressed, however, Northern fears of black immigration subsided—thanks, in large part, to the skillful leadership of the federal government. President Lincoln was among those who pointed out that freed slaves probably would prefer to stay in the South. Supporters of emancipation argued that it was bondage, not freedom, that drove slaves north. Once slavery was abolished in the South, they said, the numbers of blacks moving north should diminish. This theory fitted well with a popular anti-black argument that was articulated by Albert G. Porter, a congressman from Indiana—one of the Northern states that was least accommodating to African Americans. Porter argued that in abolishing slavery his state had, in effect, elected to be a white state. Furthermore, the Southern states, by virtue of their retaining slavery, had made a choice that required them to keep their black residents. Porter's remarks typified the growing Northern attitude that black people were a Southern problem.

The increased movement of blacks from the South to the North during the Civil War helped to harden white attitudes against them, with a resulting increase in racial discrimination—which typically manifested in hardened forms of segregation. In New York City, for example, white streetcar conductors did not hesitate to vent their hostility by ejecting black passengers. Throughout the North, African Americans found it increasingly difficult to deal with whites.

Rarely, however, did African Americans accept such treatment without a fight. As the numbers of blacks serving in the Union's armed forces increased, black leaders spoke out more forcefully against racial discrimination. Some of their protests against segregation were successful. In 1864 African Americans in Chicago formed an association to oppose Illinois's black laws, and they campaigned against the city's segregated schools. A Chicago tailor named John Jones led successful fights against the state's exclusionary law and against the exclusion of black testimony in court. By the end of 1864 most of the Midwestern states had repealed their exclusionary laws—partly because of African-American pressure and partly because Northern fears of a black influx from the South had subsided by then.

In Philadelphia, William Still—a veteran abolitionist—took his fight against segregated streetcars to the state legislature. In Rhode Island, George T. Downing led the fight to desegregate public schools. African Americans in Detroit won a suit to end school segregation. Meanwhile, John Mercer Langston organized branches of the Equal Rights League across the country, and Frederick Douglass led the National Convention of Colored Citizens of the United States. In January 1865 African Americans in Michigan and Indiana petitioned their state legislatures for relief from discriminatory laws. Throughout the North blacks sought freer admission to schools, churches, and public transportation.

Shortly before the Civil War ended, a black New York City clergyman named Henry Highland Garnet spoke before the House of Representatives. He expressed the frustrations of African Americans in universal terms:

> It is often asked when and where will the demands of the reformers of this and coming ages end? It is a fair question, and I will answer.
>
> When all the unjust and heavy burdens shall be removed from every man in the land. When all invidious and proscriptive distinctions shall be blotted out from our laws, whether they be constitutional, statute, or municipal laws. When emancipation shall be followed by enfranchisement, and all men holding allegiance to the government shall enjoy every right of American citizenship. When our brave and gallant soldiers shall have justice done unto them. When the men who endure the sufferings and perils of the battlefield in the defense of their country, and in order to keep our rulers in their places, shall enjoy the well-earned privilege of voting for them. When in the army and navy, and in every legitimate and honorable occupation, promotion shall smile upon merit without the slightest regard to the complexion of a man's face. When there shall be no more class-legislation, and no more trouble concerning the black man and his rights, than there is in regard to other American citizens. When, in every respect, he shall be equal before the law, and shall be left to make his own way in the social walks of life.

In addition to the large numbers of black soldiers who fought, black civilians worked hard to support the Lincoln Administration. They also lobbied the administration to support the principle of equal suffrage, and they pushed political leaders at all levels of government to support the Union cause and their own right to vote. Freedom without the vote, they argued, meant little. By the end of the war, however, only six states allowed blacks to vote: Maine, New Hampshire, Massachusetts, Rhode Island, Vermont, and New York. Their combined African-American population was only 65,000 people (75 percent of whom lived in New York)—a figure representing only 1.5 percent of the black population of the country as a whole.

As it became clear that a likely outcome of the Civil War would be emancipation of all the slaves in the South, the question of what to do with them was increasingly debated. The war gave a new impetus to the old idea of colonization. This took segregation to its ultimate conclusion: Instead of merely excluding black people from certain parts of the country, they would be sent out of the United States altogether. The North's ruling Republican Party officially supported voluntary colonization as an alternative to having blacks migrate north. Some Republican members of Congress even acknowledged such motives openly. In July 1862 President Lincoln told his cabinet that he was about to issue an executive order to promote colonization schemes. He never issued the order, but he did encourage black leaders to support colonization.

Africa was the primary place to which white supporters of colonization looked, but other, closer sites were also considered. In 1862, for example, an assistant secretary of the interior proposed settling former American slaves at a place known as Chiriqui, in what is now northwestern Panama in Central America. Later that year, Lincoln's cabinet considered settling blacks in Florida. This scheme was soon set aside, however, when Lincoln arranged for a private contractor to send 5,000 African Americans to an island off the coast of Haiti. Four hundred people actually went there in early 1863, but the scheme failed miserably, and its survivors were glad for the chance simply to return home.

Despite this failure, the Lincoln Administration did not give up completely on colonization as a partial solution of the problem of what to do with emancipated slaves. To help

In early 1866, shortly after the Thirteenth Amendment abolished slavery throughout the United States, thousands of African Americans gathered in the District of Columbia to celebrate the great event. (Courtesy Library of Congress, Prints and Photographs Division)

with the deportation of slaves that were expected to be freed, the government moved to recognize the sovereignty of both Liberia and Haiti. After the United States formally recognized Haiti in November 1864, the latter's President Fabre Nicolas Geffrard announced his plan to bring "industrious men of African descent from the United States."

Meanwhile, by early 1863 Lincoln's administration was working on a plan to keep freed slaves in the South. Thousands of them wished to leave the region, but most remained there. Despite the fact that the government was then anxious for settlers to help develop its vast western territories, no one encouraged black people to go there. What the Lincoln administration did instead was try to improve conditions in the South to discourage black emigration to the North. It also hoped to put former slaves to work to help the military cause.

The evident success of the Lincoln administration's emancipation policy during the Civil War raised the popularity of the Republican Party in the North. Lincoln was reelected in 1864, and Republicans increased their strength in Congress. Armed with a powerful mandate, Republican Party leaders pushed through a constitutional amendment that would abolish slavery in America once and for all. On January 31, 1865, Congress sent this amendment to the states for ratification. In mid-December—eight months after the war ended—the Thirteenth Amendment was ratified, and slavery was finally outlawed throughout the country. The war was over and the slaves were freed, but the nation still faced the monumental task or healing its war wounds and finding a place for the slaves in American society.

NOTES

pp. 68–69 "there is a physical difference . . ." Quoted in C. Vann Woodward, *The Strange Career of Jim Crow*, p. 21.

p. 70 "Henceforth let the war cry . . ." Quoted in W. A. Low and V. A. Clift, *Encyclopedia of Black America* (New York: Da Capo, 1981), p. 64.

p. 72 "The question is . . ." Quoted in V. Jacque Voegeli, *Free but Not Equal* (Chicago: University of Chicago Press, 1967), p. 99.

p. 76 "Inexperienced officers . . ." Quoted in Fisher and Quarles, *The Negro American: A Documentary History*, p. 233.

p. 79 "It is often asked . . ." Quoted in Low and Clift, *Encyclopedia of Black America*, p. 67.

6

Reconstruction

$\mathcal{A}$fter the Confederate commander in chief, Robert E. Lee, surrendered to Northern general Ulysses S. Grant on April 9, 1865, the question of whether the South could secede from the Union was answered definitively: It could not. The North's military victory preserved the Union, but it still remained for the shattered South to rejoin the nation. President Lincoln had provided a clue about how this world be done in his second inaugural address, which he delivered a month before the war ended. In that speech he refused to blame the South for the war. Instead, he called for a postwar reconciliation "with malice toward none, with charity for all." However, Lincoln was assassinated a week after the war ended.

Inclined to be generous toward the South, Lincoln had allowed Louisiana, Tennessee, and Arkansas to rejoin the

Union even before the war ended. However, four years of bitter and destructive fighting left the Northern Republicans who controlled Congress after the war in anything but a charitable mood toward the South. Many Republican members of Congress regarded Lincoln's Reconstruction plan as too lenient, and they objected to its failure to provide adequate protections for freed slaves. In mid-1864 Radical Republicans drove a bill for a harsher Reconstruction plan through Congress. Lincoln vetoed the bill and was in the process of revising his own plan when he was killed.

The fact that a Southerner killed the president further increased Northern anger toward the South. Many Northern politicians wanted to punish the South. One way they could do this was by raising the political and social condition of blacks to the same level as that of Southern whites. There were Northerners who sincerely wanted to improve the condition of African Americans for the simple, humanitarian reason that it was the right thing to do; however, both self-interest and revenge against the South played roles in Reconstruction policy. The fact that if given the vote Southern blacks would almost certainly vote for the Republican Party was not overlooked, either. Some Northerners had an additional selfish motive for helping newly freed African Americans: Improving the condition of former slaves in the South would leave them with less reason for migrating north, where they were not welcome. Through the tumultuous changes of Reconstruction, African Americans were pawns in the unresolved conflict between North and South.

Reconstruction began formally in March 1867, when Congress divided most of the former Confederacy into five military districts. However, the process of rebuilding began before the war even ended. For practical purposes, Reconstruction started as early as March 1865, when the Freedmen's Bureau was established. Through the two years immediately following the end of the war, federal policy toward the South went through several major changes, partly because of a power struggle going on in Washington between the Congress and the presidency. Eventually, however, federal policy toward the South eventually became that of victorious conquerors occupying the country of the vanquished. During the decade that formal Reconstruction lasted, federal troops forced the former Confederate states to comply with the new order, which insisted—among other things—that blacks be allowed to register and vote in large numbers. At the same time, the federal government suspended some of the civil liberties of supporters of the former Confederacy.

It is difficult to overstate the magnitude of the changes that Reconstruction brought to Southern blacks. One of the great experiments in American history, it was also one of the nation's most hopeful eras. After the Civil War nearly 4 million African Americans rose from having virtually no political rights to having, not only full rights of citizenship, but significant political power. Through this period, Congress passed seven civil rights acts—including five with long-term significance—and it pushed through three of the most important amendments to the Constitution: the Thirteenth Amendment (1865) outlawed slavery; the Fourteenth Amendment (1868) gave citizenship to all blacks; and the Fifteenth Amendment (1870) secured the right to vote for African Americans. In 1875 Congress broadened civil rights protections of African Americans by passing a sweeping civil rights act promising all Americans equal access to public accommodations and transportation.

Not only did newly freed blacks suddenly have the vote; they were in the majority in some electoral districts. This was due to the fact that the right to vote was temporarily taken away from about 150,000 Southern whites, and other whites were reluctant to vote in the early years of Reconstruction. As a result, blacks were elected to many public offices.

After the ratification of the Thirteenth Amendment, the year 1865 ended with slavery no longer permitted anywhere in the country. For the first time in two centuries abolition was not the highest priority for black Americans. What was most important now—particularly in the devastated South—was survival. Satisfying the elemental needs of food, shelter, and clothing, and protecting one's family and property counted for a great deal and questions of desegregation for little. In February 1866 a group of African-American leaders met with President Andrew Johnson—the first such meeting of its kind. They summed up the political discontentment that blacks were then experiencing in this way:

> Our coming is a marked circumstance, noting determined hope that we are not satisfied with an amendment prohibiting slavery, but that we wish it enforced with appropriate legislation. . . . We see no recognition of color or race in the organic law of the land. It knows no privileged class, and therefore we cherish the hope that we may be fully enfranchised, not only here in this District, but throughout the land. We respectfully submit that rendering anything less than this will rendering to us less than our just due; that granting anything less than our full rights will be a disregard of our just rights and of due respect for our feelings.

Johnson replied that questions of suffrage should be left to the states, not the federal government—an answer that merely added to the dissatisfactions of those seeking change.

Immediately after becoming president, Johnson adopted the most generous elements of Lincoln's Reconstruction plan, allowing all the rebel states to rejoin the Union quickly. Dominated by former Confederate leaders, the South's reconstituted state governments wasted no time in legislating codes limiting the freedoms of blacks. South Carolina, for example, enacted a detailed set of regulations governing the conduct of all African Americans—just three days after the Thirteenth Amendment was ratified in December 1865. Known as "black codes"—like their older Northern counterparts—these Southern laws made some concessions to the legal freedom of blacks by permitting them to own property, make contracts, conduct suits in court, and have valid marriage bonds. On the whole, however, the laws were designed to take away the freedom of former slaves. Such laws uniformly prohibited African Americans from serving on juries, bearing arms, or participating in mass meetings. The laws' educational provisions mandated segregated schools.

In addition to restricting the liberties and mobility of all black people within state borders, the black codes imposed terms for the relationships among African Americans and their white employers that differed little from conditions under slavery. Many codes also severely restricted the occupations in which African Americans could engage. Under South Carolina's black code, for example:

> No person of color shall pursue or practice the art, trade or business of an artisan, mechanic or shop-keeper, or any other trade, employment or business (besides that of husbandry, or that of a servant under a contract for service or labor) on his own account and for his own benefit, or in partnership with a white person, or as agent or servant of any person, until he shall have obtained a license therefor from the Judge of the District Court, which license shall be good for one year only.

The South's new black codes incensed many Northerners, who resented seeing their former enemies make a mockery of the abolition of slavery. When Congress convened in December 1865, representatives of eight additional Southern states appeared, demanding admission for the first time since their states had seceded. Northern legislators were appalled by the fact that these new Southern delegations included numerous former high-ranking Confederate political and military officers. After refusing to admit any of these delegations, Congress created a joint committee to devise a new plan for restoring the Southern states to the Union.

Congress's search for a better system of restoring rebel states to the Union, along with unanswered questions about the constitutionality of the Civil Rights Act that it passed in 1866, prompted Republican legislators to draft another constitutional amendment that would settle all these issues once and for all. The Fourteenth Amendment that they framed laid down strict ground rules for restoration of statehood to the Southern states, and Congress made its ratification a condition for each state's readmittance. President Johnson opposed every Reconstruction initiative that Congress took; the resulting battle between the legislative and executive branches developed into one of the most bitter in U.S. history. Eventually it would lead to Congress's impeachment of Johnson. Meanwhile, Congress pushed ahead with its own Reconstruction plans.

After being strengthened by the 1866 elections, the radical Republicans pushed several strong Reconstruction measures through Congress in 1867. The boldest of these declared that all the states of the former Confederacy—except Tennessee, the only Southern state to ratify the Fourteenth Amendment—no longer existed. In their place, five military districts were created, each under the command of a Northern army general. It was generally acknowledged that the Constitution did not permit Congress to dictate suffrage requirements to "states"; however, since these new military districts technically were not states, Congress ordered federal registrars to register *all* adult males—without regard to their color. Under the congressional Reconstruction plan, the newly registered voters were to elect provincial delegates to conventions that were to frame new state constitutions—which had to include provisions guaranteeing the vote to African Americans. After voters at large ratified these constitutions, elections would be held to set up new state governments. Finally, once the newly elected legislatures ratified the Fourteenth Amend-

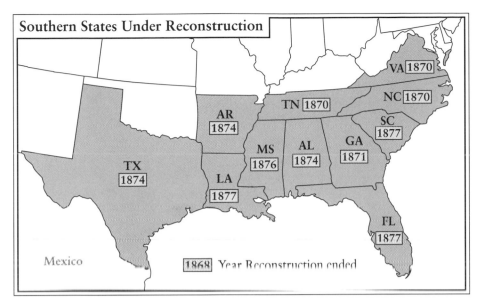

Southern States Under Reconstruction

VA 1870
TN 1870
NC 1870
AR 1874
SC 1877
MS 1876
AL 1874
GA 1871
TX 1874
LA 1877
FL 1877
Mexico
1868 Year Reconstruction ended

Harsh Union Reconstruction policies attempted to force racial equality on the South after the Civil War but instead embittered white Southerners, leaving a disastrous legacy for the region's large African-American population.

ment and Congress approved their new constitutions, the states could be readmitted. Six states completed this process by the end of 1868; the rest followed over the next 18 months.

Under the supervision of federal troops, large numbers of African Americans registered to vote through the summer of 1867. At the end of this first great registration drive, black voters were the majority within Alabama, Florida, Louisiana, Mississippi, and South Carolina, as well as an overall majority in the South as a whole. As a result, they were able to participate in the framing of the new state constitutions and in filling elected offices.

In a broad sense, it might be said that "Reconstruction" began in the South whenever and wherever Union troops occupied Confederate territory and proclaimed martial law —a process that began in the first year of the Civil War. However, the first concerted effort to apply uniform occupation policies occurred in March 1865, when the federal government created the Bureau of Refugees, Freedmen, and Abandoned Lands as a branch of the War Department. This agency was designed to look after the needs of all people displaced by the war in occupied Southern territories, but it was mostly closely associated with the assistance that it provided to former slaves. For this reason it was known as the "Freedmen's Bureau." Despite the fact that powerful factions in the government—including President Johnson—opposed its efforts, the bureau established itself as an effective relief agency. By the middle of 1865 the bureau was supplying food, medical care, clothing, and shelter to hundreds of thousands of African Americans, and it was putting freed slaves to work in abandoned plantations and as military laborers.

In July 1866 Congress expanded the bureau's mission by charging it with responsibility for protecting the rights of former slaves and helping them to become self-supporting citizens. One way in which it attempted to carry out this mission was in helping African Americans to become landowners. A few thousand black families obtained land through the bureau's efforts, but in the absence of adequate congressional support the bureau had little impact in this regard. The government's failure to give former slaves a substantial share of property would leave them permanently vulnerable to more prosperous landowning whites, and it would contribute significantly to later black migrations out of the South—which was precisely what the federal government wished to prevent when it created the bureau.

Meanwhile, the bureau made a more lasting contribution to the South by beginning a public education system for African Americans. In developing educational institutions where none had existed before, the bureau had little interest in integration. Its primary mission was simply to get blacks into classrooms—which it did. By 1870 nearly ¼ million African Americans were attending more than 4,200 bureau-created schools. Most of these were racially segregated—

thereby contributing to what would later become one of the most deeply entrenched institutions of segregation. During Reconstruction the laws of only two states, Louisiana and South Carolina, specifically mandated nonsegregated schools, but it was only in New Orleans that anything resembling significant school integration was achieved.

The bureau also contributed to the developing tradition of all-black colleges by helping to start what became Fisk University in Nashville, Tennessee, and Atlanta University in Georgia. Another black college, Howard University—which was chartered in Washington, D.C., in 1867—took its name from the bureau's first commissioner, Oliver Otis Howard.

The Freedmen's Bureau played a major role in providing relief to the war-torn South, but it was less successful in its mission of helping blacks win their new rights as citizens. The federal government gradually lost interest in the bureau and finally abolished it in July 1872. After helping to register hundreds of thousands of black voters, the bureau did little to secure full citizenship rights for African Americans. Its

In creating public education systems for newly freed slaves where none had existed before, the Freedmen's Bureau unintentionally laid the groundwork for segregated schools throughout the South. (Arkent Archive)

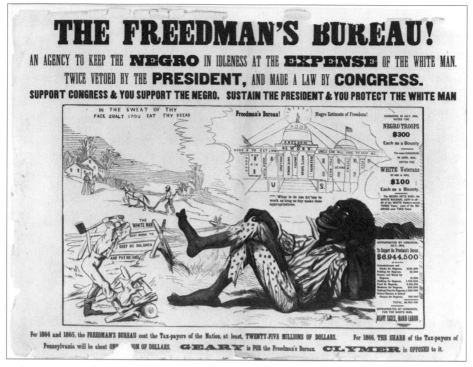

When Hiester Clymer ran for governor of Pennsylvania against John White Geary in 1866, he appealed to Northern resentment of the Freedmen's Bureau by charging Geary—who had been military governor of Savannah, Georgia—with supporting the bureau's work. Although Geary won the election, the charges that Clymer leveled against the bureau in this campaign poster were early indications that Northern support of Reconstruction would be short-lived. (Courtesy Library of Congress, Prints and Photographs Division)

main legacy was the creation of an educational system, but one that would remain segregated for a century.

Despite the fact that black voters held majorities in many parts of the South during Reconstruction, they never won elective offices in proportion to their numbers. Nevertheless, they were elected to more offices in the South than they would hold anywhere in the country until well over a century later. Several states sent black representatives to Congress, and Mississippi sent two black senators. Most black politicians served in state and local governments. The closest

African Americans came to controlling a state was in South Carolina, where they briefly held a majority of the lower house of the legislature. (South Carolina was also the only state in which an African American sat on a supreme court.)

Despite the severely limited educational opportunities of black politicians before emancipation and their complete lack of political experience, most of them performed well. Many distinguished themselves with the breadth of their vision, in looking beyond their own interests to work for the general betterment of their states. Mississippi's black senators, Blanche Kelso Bruce and Hiram R. Revels (who served at different times), both worked, not only to advance the rights of African Americans, but also to restore the rights taken away from former white Confederates.

Mississippi provides a good illustration of how Reconstruction brought profound political changes to the South. A majority of its registered voters in 1867 were black. The following year a constitutional convention met, with 17 African Americans among its 100 representatives. When Mississippi's first legislature under its new constitution sat two years later, a quarter of the 140 legislators in both houses were black. Over the next four years, this biracial government reorganized the state university, and it created a biracial state educational system, which included two black teaching colleges and a black university. It also repealed all the state's racially discriminatory laws and affirmed the right of all citizens to use desegregated public accommodations.

While Southern blacks were playing active roles in government, virtually no African Americans in the

> We want mixed schools not because our colored schools are inferior to white schools—not because colored instructors are inferior to white instructors, but because we want to do away with a system that exalts one class and debases another.
>
> ◆
>
> —Frederick Douglass, editorial in the New National Era, May 2, 1872

North were elected to public offices. Indeed, one of the great ironies of the Reconstruction era was that African Americans in the South—most of whom had been slaves until a few years earlier—suddenly enjoyed more civil liberties than Northern blacks who had been free for several generations. When the Civil War ended, the only Northern states to grant unrestricted voting rights to blacks were Maine, Massachusetts, New Hampshire, Rhode Island, Vermont, and Wisconsin. As late as 1868, Kansas, Michigan, Minnesota, and Ohio all rejected African-American suffrage.

The war years had seen some lifting of the black codes in Northern states, but the overall improvement in the condition of Northern blacks was slight. In Northern states, African Americans were still either denied the vote outright, or—occassionally—they had to meet property qualifications not required of white voters. They could not serve in state militias, and institutions of segregation generally circumscribed their lives. Most public schools in the North were segregated, and some states—such as Indiana and Illinois—had no schools at all for black children.

Most Northern blacks lived in cities, where their opportunities for employment were severely restricted by segregated hiring practices. Regardless of their skills, African Americans were generally limited to working at unskilled trades and in menial service. A number of occupations would eventually become closely identified with African Americans: waiters, servants, barbers, washerwomen, hod carriers, and porters. Barred from white labor unions, African Americans often tried to form their own unions.

Nonetheless, much of the Reconstruction legislation enacted to improve conditions for newly free slaves also helped to improve conditions for Northern blacks, to some extent. In March and April 1866 Congress passed the first of a series of civil rights acts. Written to counter the discriminatory black codes of the Southern states, the 1866 act was the first federal law specifically to forbid states from discriminating against citizens on account of race. Its language was clear:

> . . . all persons born in the United States and not subject to any foreign power, excluding Indians not taxed, are hereby declared to be citizens of the United States; and such citizens, of every race and color, without regard to any previous condition of slavery or involuntary servitude, except as a punishment for crime whereof the party shall have been duly convicted, shall have the same right, in every State and Territory in the United States, to make and enforce contracts, to sue, be parties, and give evidence, to inherit, purchase, lease, sell, hold, and convey real and personal property, and to full and equal benefit of all laws and proceedings for the security of person and property, as is enjoyed by white citizens . . .

Taking a narrow states' rights position, President Johnson vetoed the bill, but Congress overrode his veto.

In 1866 Congress passed a civil rights act that granted citizenship to all African Americans, but Congress's authority to do so was questionable. Therefore, Republicans in Congress pushed through another amendment to the Constitution that, not only settled this issue, but also spelled out requirements for rebel states to reenter the Union. In the matter of citizenship, the language of the Fourteenth Amendment was unequivocal: "All persons born or naturalized in the United States, and subject to the jurisdiction thereof, are citizens of the United States and of the State wherein they reside." Ratification of that single sentence finally put the question of African-American citizenship beyond the reach of any legal challenge. The amendment contained additional clauses of almost equal significance to African Americans:

> No State shall make or enforce any law which shall abridge the privileges or immunities of citizens of the United States; nor shall any State deprive any person of

life, liberty, or property, without due process of law; nor deny to any person within its jurisdiction the equal protection of the laws.

Twentieth-century court interpretations of these clauses would make this amendment one of the most important weapons in the civil rights movement. At the time the amendment was ratified, however, their impact was limited.

As radical Republican Reconstruction policies forced the South to enfranchise African Americans, the question naturally arose of why blacks in the South should be able to vote, while many in the North could not. To answer this question, Congress framed the Fifteenth Amendment. It specifically guaranteed: "The right of citizens of the United States to vote shall not be denied or abridged by the United States or by any state on account of race, color, or previous condition of

Ratification of the Fifteenth Amendment in early 1870 guaranteed African-American men the right to vote. Fully understanding the significance of this event, thousands of black Civil War veterans marched through New York City to celebrate. (Courtesy Library of Congress, Prints and Photographs Division)

servitude." Congress added ratification of this amendment to the list of conditions that unreconstructed Southern states had to meet in order to be readmitted to the Union, but the amendment was far from popular outside of the South. Indeed, it took Southern votes to ratify it, because it was rejected by California, Delaware, Kentucky, Maryland, Oregon, and Tennessee.

One might think that language as clear as that of the Fifteenth Amendment should have settled the issue of black voting rights, but it did not. Two months after the amendment was ratified, Congress passed another major piece of civil rights legislation, the Enforcement Act, which defined criminal penalties for anyone who interfered with another person's right to vote. Congress extended this protection the following year with a civil rights law known as the "Ku Klux Klan Act," directed against anyone who tried to deprive any person or class of persons from enjoying the equal protection of the laws, as provided by the Fourteenth Amendment. Even these laws did not suffice to guarantee blacks voting rights, however.

The last grand gesture of the Reconstruction era was the Republican Party's passage of the national Civil Rights Act of 1875. This ambitious piece of legislation outlawed segregation in most public transportation, accommodations, and public amusements and guaranteed African Americans the right to serve on juries. However, the law was too rarely enforced to have a significant impact. Before the bill was passed, even more sweeping desegregation provisions were removed from it. Its original draft called for integrating schools and cemeteries. Nevertheless, what remained was powerfully worded:

> . . . all persons within the jurisdiction of the United States shall be entitled to the full and equal enjoyment of the accommodations, advantages, facilities, and privileges of inns, public conveyances on land or water,

theaters, and other places of public amusement; subject only to the conditions and limitations established by law, and applicable alike to citizens of every race and color, regardless of any previous condition of servitude.

Almost as quickly as Congress passed new civil rights legislation, opponents attempted to overturn the laws in court. Congress tried to deter judicial opposition to the laws by restating their fundamental principles in successive amendments, but tougher judicial challenges were to come. In 1873 the Supreme Court heard a series of cases known collectively as the Slaughter-House Cases, which concerned Louisiana's granting one slaughterhouse a virtual monopoly over livestock butchering in the New Orleans area. These cases were not directly related to racial discrimination, but the ruling that the Court handed down established a crucial interpretation of the privileges and immunities clause in the Fourteenth Amendment. In asserting that this amendment protected only the privileges of *national* citizenship, the Court effectively ruled that the federal government had no authority to control privileges relating to *state* citizenship. Because the kinds of rights most important to African Americans—such as equal access to public conveyances, accommodations, and education—were considered to be privileges controlled by the states, the Slaughter-House decision left the federal government with little real authority over matters relating to racial discrimination.

A second blow to the Fourteenth Amendment came in an 1876 Supreme Court ruling. The case concerned the convictions of several white men who participated in a mob action that had killed two blacks

No one asks, *no one seeks the passage of a law that will interfere with anyone's private affairs. But I do ask the enactment of a law to secure me in the enjoyment of public privileges.*

◆

—James T. Rapier,
speech to Congress, 1873

while breaking up a meeting called to discuss a Louisiana election. In *United States v. Cruikshank* the Court ruled that the Fourteenth Amendment protected citizens only against encroachments on their rights by the states themselves—and not against actions of private citizens. (The *Cruikshank* decision also declared that the Constitution did not grant rights such as the right of free assembly; it only forbade Congress itself to encroach on such rights.) Court decisions such as these whittled away the political gains that African Americans had made under Reconstruction, and more were to come.

Among the most forward-looking social developments during the Reconstruction era were efforts to build multiracial political movements in several Southern states that would replace the Northern-dominated Republican Party. The most significant of these was the Louisiana Unification Movement. Under the leadership of Confederate war hero General Pierre Beauregard, the movement sought to end Reconstruction in the state by creating a government that recognized the full civil rights of all its citizens. Beauregard not only called for ending segregation in public conveyances and accommodations and in the schools but also for dropping all color bars in employment and in corporate boards. This movement attracted significant support from New Orleans business leaders, newspapers, and planters in southern Louisiana, but its civil rights position was too advanced for most white Louisianans. All such movements failed, leaving progressive white Southerners to drift back into the pro-segregationist Democratic Party, which would soon control all the state governments.

Reconstruction formally ended in 1877, after Rutherford B. Hayes became president. However, its real end came earlier in most Southern states, and Tennessee escaped Reconstruction altogether. As early as 1870, white Democrats regained control of the state governments of Virginia and North Carolina. Georgia followed the next year; Alabama, Arkansas, and Texas in 1874; and Mississippi in 1876. Only

A Clergyman on Civil Rights

While Congress was considering the Civil Rights Act of 1875, R. H. Cain, a black South Carolina clergyman and politician, testified on the bill before a Senate committee His remarks expressed what was likely the majority view of African Americans at that time:

> Mr. Speaker, I regard the civil-rights bill as among the best measures that ever came before Congress. Why, sir, it is at the very foundation of good government. I take a higher view of the question than that of prejudice between the two classes. I regard this five million of men, women and children in the country as an integral part of the country, interwoven with all its interests. . . .
>
>   Let the laws of the country be just; let the laws of the country be equitable; that is all we ask, and we will take our chances under the laws in this land. We do not want the laws of this country to make discriminations between us. Place all citizens upon one broad platform and if the negro is not qualified to hoe his row in this contest of life, then let him go down. All we ask of this country is to put no barriers between us, to lay no stumbling blocks in our way, to give us freedom to accomplish our destiny, that we may thus acquire all that is necessary to our interest and welfare in this country. Do this, sir, and we shall ask nothing more.◆

in Florida, Louisiana, and South Carolina did whites have to wait until 1877 to retake control of their state governments. In any case, direct military rule ended entirely in 1870 and it ended two years earlier in every state but Mississippi, Texas, and Virginia.

While governments of some Southern states such as Mississippi made sincere efforts to make Reconstruction work, most white Southerners refused to accept the new order. They learned to accept their defeat in the Civil War, and they were learning to accept the abolition of slavery; however, they

The national convention movement was an important part of African-American civil rights activities through the 19th century. At the 1876 convention held in Nashville, Tennessee, pictured here, delegates considered problems associated with the imminent end of Reconstruction. (Arkent Archive)

were not ready to accept social and political equality with African Americans. If necessary, they were prepared to turn to violence to prevent it. Groups such as the Ku Klux Klan instituted reigns of terror in Mississippi and elsewhere that made a shambles of black political gains. White violence and threats of violence drove African Americans away from the polls and terrorized the schools. In the decades that followed, racial discrimination and segregation would become defining characteristics of the South.

Despite its ultimate failure, Reconstruction left some positive legacies. In addition to the revolutionary constitutional amendments that it forged, it brought major political reforms to state governments in the South. The new constitutions that Southern states were forced to frame brought radical improvements in judicial systems, administrative procedures, methods of taxation, and electoral systems. Reconstruction also accelerated the development of widespread free public education. Virtually all the awkward experiments made to end segregation during Reconstruction were short lived, but the more fundamental advances of the era laid the foundation for the modern civil rights movement.

One of the ironies of Reconstruction was the effect it had on the North. Reconstruction policies were often initiated by Northern politicians who had little interest in improving conditions for Northern blacks. However, the changes that they set in motion in the South generally also led to improvements in the North. After Reconstruction ended, the gains in political conditions that Southern blacks were enjoying soon disappeared, but Northern blacks continued to enjoy most of their own gains.

NOTES

p. 86 "Our coming . . ." Quoted in Fishel and Quarles, *The Negro American: A Documentary History*, p. 275.

p. 87 "No person of color . . ." Quoted in Albert P. Blaustein and Robert L. Zangrando, *Civil Rights and the Black American: A Documentary History*, pp. 223–24.

p. 95 "all persons . . ." Quoted in Blaustein and Zangrando, *Civil Rights and the Black American: A Documentary History* (New York: Clarion Books, 1970), p. 230.

p. 98 "all persons within . . ." Quoted in Blaustein and Zangrando, *Civil Rights and the Black American: A Documentary History*, p. 241.

p. 100 "Mr. Speaker, . . ." Quoted in Fishel and Quarles, *The Negro American: A Documentary History*, pp. 286, 288–89.

7

"Separate but Equal"

The United States celebrated its centennial in 1876. The year was more than just a symbolic moment in the nation's history. It brought real political and social changes that would have a lasting impact on African Americans. By that time the North was weary of Reconstruction and anxious to turn its attention elsewhere. Lakota chief Sitting Bull's forces' annihilation of George Armstrong Custer's Seventh Cavalry at Little Big Horn in June 1876 awakened Americans to the need to bring the vast Western frontier under control so that westward expansion could continue unimpeded. The same day that the Lakota and Cheyenne crushed Custer, Alexander Graham Bell was at a Centennial Exposition in Philadelphia, demonstrating his telephone—an invention symbolizing the technological changes that were about to transform America from an agricultural nation into an urban industrial giant. This change, too, was a vital one for African Americans, whose future lay in the cities.

Meanwhile, European immigrants were pouring into America in unprecedented numbers, crowding into Northern cities where they competed with African Americans for jobs and housing. Blacks were already a minority in America. Their numbers were growing rapidly, but even more rapid European immigration ensured that their proportion of the nation's total population would shrink, not grow. During the 1870s alone, more than 11 million Europeans came to America—nearly double the number of black Americans already resident in the country.

The 1876 presidential election brought one of the most decisive changes in American history. Despite the political changes of the Reconstruction era, most former Confederate states were already back under the control of Southern whites. With the restoration of Southern white voters, the Democratic Party was once again strong enough to challenge for the White House. Samuel J. Tilden, the Democratic candidate in 1876, won a clear majority in the national popular vote, but he fell a single electoral vote short of winning the presidency outright. Rutherford B. Hayes, the candidate of the Republican Party—which had designed and controlled Reconstruction—was 20 electoral votes short of victory. Exactly this same number of votes was disputed because of charges of electoral fraud in the last Southern states still controlled by Reconstruction Republicans—South Carolina, Florida, and Louisiana.

The disputed election left the country without a president-elect from November 1876 until late February 1877, when an electoral commission awarded all 20 disputed votes to Hayes. With the presidency at stake, it was a nervous time— one in which the possibility of renewed Civil War was real. Within the electoral commission, Republican members had a one-vote advantage over Democrats, so there was no doubt which way the commission's decision would go. The only real question was how the Republicans could get Southern Democrats to accept their candidate as president. The solution was a deal known as the "Great Compromise." In return for being allowed to place Hayes in office without a fight, the Republicans pledged to end Reconstruction by removing the last federal troops from the South. They also pledged to appoint a Southerner to the president's cabinet and to help subsidize economic development in the South.

The Great Compromise thus abandoned the South's African Americans to their former masters—who still seethed over the Civil War and the humiliations of Reconstruction. The only thing Republicans did was ask the Democrats for a verbal promise to treat blacks fairly. Soon after President Hayes was inaugurated, he upheld his party's pledge to the Democrats by withdrawing the last federal troops from the South. In late April Louisiana became the last Southern state to regain local control of its government, and Reconstruction officially ended. The change had little to do with Hayes himself, however. Reconstruction almost certainly would have ended around this same time without him.

The end of Reconstruction unleashed a wave of white violence against African Americans. Unchecked by federal troops, white groups such as the Ku Klux Klan began a campaign of terror to keep blacks from voting or attempting to exercise their rights. *Lynching* became a disturbingly familiar word, as white mobs tortured, hanged, and burned blacks. Their purpose was not to exact justice for any real crimes but to avenge their own humiliations by terrorizing black people. By the 1890s, lynchings were claiming the lives of black men at a rate of one every two days.

In the face of poverty and repression, many African Americans saw their own salvation in leaving the South. They began a northward and westward migration that continued until well into the 20th century. The fears that Southern blacks felt launched a spontaneous surge of emigration

Lynching

Black Mississippi journalist Ida B. Wells Barnett described the nightmare in which African Americans found themselves at the end of Reconstruction, when violence against blacks and lynching were common:

> The government that had made the Negro a citizen found itself unable to protect him. It gave him the right to vote, but denied him the protection that should have maintained that right. Scourged from his home; hunted through the swamps; hung by midnight raiders, and openly murdered in the light of day, the Negro clung to his right of franchise with a heroism that would have wrung admiration from the hearts of savages. He believed that in the small white ballot there was a subtle something that stood for manhood as well as citizenship, and thousands of brave black men went to their graves, exemplifying the one by dying for the other.◆

We had much rather stayed there [in the South] if we could have had our rights. . . . In 1877 we lost all hopes . . . we found ourselves in such condition that we looked around and we seed that there was no way on earth, it seemed, that we could better our condition there . . .

◆

—Exoduster Henry Adams, testimony to U.S. Senate committee (1879)

in 1879 that became known as the "Exodus of 1879." Tens of thousands of people went west—mostly to Kansas, where they were dubbed "Exodusters." Many followed leaders such as Benjamin "Pap" Singleton, a former Tennessee slave who preached black separatism. Some dreamed of making the undeveloped territory that later became Oklahoma an all-black state. However, most migrants simply found new hardships on the frontier, as well as familiar forms of discrimination. States such as California lacked the South's increasingly discriminatory legislation but still practiced many of the same forms of segregation. In general, the farther west that African Americans migrated, the worse they were treated.

After Congress had passed the Civil Rights Act of 1875, the federal government did little to enforce its provisions against segregation in public accommodations. The end of Reconstruction made the act a dead letter in the South. In 1878 the U.S. Supreme Court even ruled in favor of a Mississippi steamboat company's protest against the state's Reconstruction-era legislation that outlawed segregation on the boats.

In 1881 Tennessee became the first state to legislate segregation on its trains. Its new law forbade black and white passengers from traveling together but required every train to offer black passengers accommodations equivalent to those for whites. This was an early example of the "separate but equal" doctrine—the peculiar idea that segregation could be compatible with equality.

The "Exodus of 1879" was the first of many large-scale movements of African Americans out of the South. Many of these people went west, hoping to find freedom in the undeveloped new territories. Generally, however, they found the same kinds of discrimination and segregation that they had experienced in the South. (Arkent Archive)

African Americans who felt that they had suffered discrimination under violations of the Civil Rights Act of 1875 began taking their complaints to court. In 1883 five cases concerning illegal segregation by innkeepers, theater owners, and a railroad company came together before the U.S. Supreme Court. The Court ruled that the Thirteenth and Fourteenth Amendments had never given Congress authority to pass the public accommodation provisions of the Civil Rights Act of 1875. Writing for the majority, Justice Joseph P. Bradley argued that the amendments did not guarantee African Americans protection against unequal treatment in the *private* domain—which included hotels, theaters, and trains. Only one justice, John Marshall Harlan—whom President Hayes had appointed—dissented. Harlan argued that the Civil Rights Act was designed expressly to combat assumptions that blacks were inferior to whites. Furthermore, he argued that inns, theaters, and trains were equivalent to the kinds of public facilities in which all citizens' constitutional rights must be protected.

Former abolitionists called the Supreme Court's anti–civil rights ruling the "new Dred Scott decision," but white public opinion generally favored it. The Court's decision killed the once-promising postwar struggle against segregation. Florida quickly copied Tennessee's segregated train laws, with other Southern states soon following suit. The Supreme Court's crushing blow to desegregation moved a young black journalist named T. Thomas Fortune to write:

> The colored people of the United States feel to-day as if they had been baptized in ice water. From Maine to Florida they are earnestly discussing the decision of the Supreme Court declaring the Civil Rights law to be unconstitutional . . .
>
> Having declared that colored men have no protection from the government in their political rights, the Supreme Court now declares that we have no civil rights —declares that railroad corporations are free to force

us into smoking cars or cattle cars; that hotel keepers are free to make us walk the streets at night; that theatre managers can refuse us admittance to their exhibitions for the amusement of the public—it has reaffirmed the infamous decision of the infamous Chief Justice Taney [author of the *Dred Scott* decision] that a "black man has no rights that a white man is bound to respect."

It would be nearly another century before Congress passed a new civil rights act. Most of the states in the Northeast and Midwest and some in the Far West passed civil rights acts of their own after the Supreme Court invalidated the federal acts. These state laws took away the legal justifications for segregation, but the laws were not always enforced with vigor. Meanwhile, the Southern states launched fresh assaults on the rights of African Americans, beginning with a drive to take away the vote that had been guaranteed them by the Fifteenth Amendment.

The Fifteenth Amendment states that the "right of citizens of the United States to vote shall not be denied or abridged by the United States or by any state on account of race, color, or previous condition of servitude." Despite the clear language of the law, blacks were still denied the franchise. If white intimidation failed to scare black voters away from the polls, then cleverly written laws disfranchised them.

In late 1890, Mississippi ratified a new constitution that required voters to pay fees known as poll taxes and to pass literacy tests. Both rules placed special burdens on black voters. Those who could afford to pay the poll tax had to do so many months before elections took place; then they had to hang on to their

> If we are not striving for equality, in heaven's name for what are we living? . . . If we cannot do what other freemen do, then we are not free. Yes, my friends, I want equality. Nothing less.
>
> ◆
>
> —John Hope, speech to a black debating society in Nashville, Tennessee, February 22, 1896

receipts until voting day. Finally, when they appeared at the polls to vote, they had to convince registrars that they could read. Since the registrars were invariably white and could interpret literacy test results as they wished, the chances of a black voter's actually being allowed to cast a vote were slim. Many white Mississippians were themselves illiterate, but they confidently could ignore such obstacles as literacy tests because of the state's clever "grandfather clause" rule. This rule guaranteed the vote to *any* man whose grandfather had voted. It was a tidy way to disqualify African Americans from voting, since none of them had grandfathers who had voted in Mississippi—or anywhere else.

In the late 1880s, Mississippi's black citizens appealed to President Benjamin Harrison for help, but he declined to interfere on the pretext that awarding of the franchise was a matter for the states to decide. The House of Representatives passed a bill to prevent these new assaults on black voting rights, but the bill died in the Senate the following year. Unhampered by the federal government, other states soon followed Mississippi's example and instituted grandfather clauses. By the early 20th century, African Americans were virtually disfranchised throughout the South. With rights diminishing, blacks turned ever more strongly to education as the path to salvation. Black educator W. E. B. Du Bois wrote of this period that

> the Revolution of 1876 came, and left the half-free serf weary, wondering but still inspired. Slowly but steadily, in the following years, a new vision began gradually to replace the dream of political power—a powerful movement, the rise of another ideal to guide the unguided, another ideal of "book-learning"; the curiosity, born of compulsory ignorance, to know and test the power of the cabalistic letters of the white man, the longing to know.

In 1881 Booker T. Washington founded Tuskegee Institute in Alabama to offer agricultural and industrial training to African Americans. Washington combined his personal drive and charisma with Tuskegee's success to become America's leading black spokesperson by the turn of the century. In September 1895 he spoke before the Cotton States International Expositions in Atlanta. His speech became an African American political manifesto for the immediate future known as the "Atlanta Compromise."

Washington renounced black aspirations for social and political equality, asking instead for black people only to have the opportunity to learn trades and make themselves economically useful. "Cast down your bucket where you are," he intoned, and be satisfied with having "a man's chance in the commercial world." He urged blacks to concentrate on learning to work with their hands before worrying about loftier goals. "It is at the bottom of life we must begin, and not at the top. Nor should we permit our grievances to overshadow our opportunities." He appealed directly to whites to look for the South's prosperity not in the labor of the multitudes of foreigners pouring into the country, but "among the eight millions of Negroes whose habits you know, whose fidelity and love you have tested . . ." He laid down a prescription for voluntary segregation by assuring whites that

> you and your families will be surrounded by the most patient, faithful, law-abiding and unresentful people that the world has seen. As we have proved our loyalty to you in the past, in nursing your children, watching by the sick-bed of your mothers and fathers, and often following them with tear-dimmed eyes to their graves, so in the future, in our humble way, we shall stand by you with a devotion that no foreigner can approach, ready to lay down our lives, if need be, in defence of yours, interlacing our industrial, commercial, civil and religious life with yours in a way that shall make the

interests of both races one. In all things that are purely social we can be as separate as the fingers, yet one as the hand in all things essential to mutual progress. . . .

The wisest among my race understand that the agitation of questions of social equality is the extremist folly, and that progress in the enjoyment of all the privileges that will come to us must be the result of severe and constant struggle rather than of artificial forcing. . . . The opportunity to earn a dollar in a factory just now is worth infinitely more than the opportunity to spend a dollar in an opera-house.

Whether Washington was consciously conceding white supremacy or cautiously trying to stave off further white-on-black violence, he articulated exactly the kind of race relations that white Southerners thought ideal. His emphasis on black self-help also impressed Northern whites, whose philanthropy was the backbone of Tuskegee.

The disapproval that many African Americans felt for Washington's Atlanta Compromise grew stronger when conditions in the South got worse instead of better. The very next year the Supreme Court made a decision that would set civil rights back for 60 years. Black citizens of Louisiana detested the state's adoption of Jim Crow rules in its railway system, which required that trains have "equal but separate accommodations for the white and colored races." Black leaders denounced the law as "unconstitutional, unamerican, unjust, dangerous and against sound policy" since it would give whites "license" to mistreat black passengers. To test the constitutionality of the system, Homer A. Plessy, a light-complexioned African American, sat in the white-only car when he rode a train out of New Orleans. When he refused to move, he was arrested. Citing his constitutional rights under the Thirteenth and Fourteenth Amendments, he took his case to the U.S. Supreme Court, which ruled against him. The central issue was whether Louisiana's law violated the Four-

Even outside of the South, Jim Crow rules were common in public transportation, as this illustration of an African American being expelled from a Pennsylvania railroad car shows. (Courtesy Library of Congress, Prints and Photographs Division)

teenth Amendment's equal protection clause. The Court's written decision contained this self-contradictory argument:

> The object of the amendment was undoubtedly to enforce the absolute equality of the two races before the

law, but, in the nature of things, it could not have been intended to abolish distinctions based upon color, or to enforce social, as distinguished from political, equality, or a commingling of the two races upon terms unsatisfactory to either.

The Court dismissed Plessy's argument

that the enforced separation of the two races stamps the colored race with a badge of inferiority. If this be so, it is not by reason of anything found in the act, but solely because the colored race chooses to put that construction on it. . . . If the two races are to meet upon terms of social equality, it must be the result [of] voluntary consent of individuals . . . Legislation is powerless to eradicate racial instincts, or to abolish distinctions based upon physical differences . . .

Once again, Hayes's appointee Justice Harlan was the lone dissenter on the Court. Citing the essential contradiction in the majority opinion's argument, he correctly pointed out that the purpose of Louisiana's Jim Crow law was not to provide "equal" accommodations but to *restrict* the personal freedom of black citizens. He went on,

The white race deems itself to be the dominant race in this country. And so it is, in prestige, in achievements, in education, in wealth, and in power. So, I doubt not, it will continue to be for all time, if it remains true to its great heritage and holds fast to the principles of constitutional liberty. But in view of the constitution, in the eye of the law, there is in this country no superior, dominant, ruling class of citizens. There is no caste here. Our constitution is color-blind.

In my opinion, the judgement this day rendered will, in time, prove to be quite as pernicious as the decision made by this tribunal in the *Dred Scott Case*. . . . [What]

can more certainly arouse race hate, what more certainly create and perpetuate a feeling of distrust between these races, than state enactments which, in fact, proceed on the ground that colored citizens are so inferior and degraded that they cannot be allowed to sit in public coaches occupied by white citizens? [The] thin disguise as "equal" accommodations for passengers in railroad coaches will not mislead any one, nor atone for the wrong this day done.

Harlan's prediction was accurate. The *Plessy* decision did prove to be as "pernicious" as the *Dred Scott* decision had

After the Civil War more than 12,000 African Americans served in all-black cavalry and infantry regiments that protected the western frontier. Known by Indians as "Buffalo Soldiers" because of their hair texture, these men did a major part of the fighting against Apaches and other Indian groups. This photograph from around 1899 shows some members of the Ninth Volunteer Infantry with their white officers. (Courtesy Library of Congress, Prints and Photographs Division)

been. In fact, it became the constitutional basis for Jim Crow throughout America. It carved in stone the idea that African-American citizens were not deprived of equal protection under the law, so long as they have access to facilities substantially "equal" to those of whites. *Plessy* defined the separate but equal doctrine for a case in the field of public transportation, but it soon spread to almost every facet of life in which people could be separated. America would enter the 20th century with the strange notion that its citizens could be segregated and equal at the same time. As the new century began Amanda Smith Jemand summed up the feelings of Southern blacks concerning segregation:

> No honest man will say we get equal if separate cars. In the drug stores we can buy poison but not a five-cent glass of soda water. We can mix bread with our hands; it is good enough to go into their stomachs, but not a penny roll can we eat in their restaurants. We can sleep in their houses, in their beds, by their sides as long as we are servants; but go into some public hostelry with money to buy our lodging in a separate room and bed, immediately we have developed a case of leprosy. We should be elevated, oh yes; but our clean, respectable boys dare not darken the doors of the Young Men's Christian Association. Public libraries are for the white public. Preachers' alliances are for white preachers. . . . We ask for no social rights. I think it is time these people knew the difference between social and civil rights. If their brains could be relieved of that phantom, I am sure they would think clearer on other subjects.

NOTES

p. 106 "The government that had . . ." *Crusade for Justice: The Autobiography of Ida B. Wells*; quoted in *Black Women in White America: A Documentary History*, ed. Gerda Lerner (New York: Vintage, 1973), p. 201.

pp. 108–109 "The colored people of the United States . . ." Quoted in Fishel and Quarles, *The Negro America: A Documentary History* (New York: Scott, Foresman, 1967), p. 315.

p. 110 "the Revolution . . ." W. E. B. Du Bois, *The Souls of Black Folk* (1903). In *Three Negro Classics* (New York: Avon Books, 1965) p. 217.

pp. 111–112 "Cast down your bucket . . ." Quoted in Fishel and Quarles, *The Negro America: A Documentary History*, pp. 343–345.

pp. 113–114 "The object of the amendment . . ." Quoted in William B. Lockhart, et al., *Constitutional Law: Cases—Comments—Questions* (6th ed., St. Paul, Minn.: West Publishing, 1986), pp. 1155–1156.

pp. 114–115 "The white race deems . . ." Quoted in Lockhart et al., *Constitutional Law*, p. 1156.

p 116 "No honest man . . ." Amanda Smith Jemand, "A Southern Woman's Appeal for Justice" (1901), quoted in *Black Women in White America*, p. 541.

8

A New Beginning:
The 20th Century

In 1901, a month after President William McKinley's assassination lifted Theodore Roosevelt to the presidency, Roosevelt invited Booker T. Washington to the White House. There they conferred and dined together. For the first time in history, an African American was a formal dinner guest in the home of the president—a fact widely noticed by both black and white Americans. Eating together had long been such a powerful taboo in black-white relations that the fact that the president actually ate at the same table as a black person had profound significance. Blacks hoped that this event signalled a new era in race relations. Many white Americans, however, were simply incensed.

What the 20th century did bring to African Americans was official abandonment of any pretense of drawing them into the mainstream of American society. The Supreme Court's 1896 *Plessy v. Ferguson* decision established a constitutional justification for all forms of segregation for the next half century. *Plessy's* benevolent-sounding "separate but equal" words seemed to reconcile contradictions that had been inherent in American democracy since Emancipation. The Constitution, it now seemed, condoned the existence of two Americas—one white and one black. While these two Americas could easily be separate, they could scarcely be equal. The South virtually disfranchised black citizens during the first years of the new century, while piling on discriminatory legislation dressed in separate-but-equal language.

In 1900 black Americans numbered nearly 9 million—most of whom lived in the rural South. Although this was more than double the number of blacks at the time of the Civil War, that figure was dwarfed by the millions of European immigrants who had come to America in the meantime. For African Americans, this flood of European immigrants was disastrous. With industry and mechanized agriculture rapidly expanding, the United States was experiencing economic growth that might have offered African Americans opportunities to join in the new prosperity. However, European immigrants took most of the new industrial jobs in the North, at the same time that farm mechanization was diminishing the value of unskilled black labor in the South. Further, as African Americans began concentrating in cities, they had to compete with immigrants for jobs as well as scarce housing.

As in the 19th century, African Americans moving into cities often faced white hostility. Some towns tried legislation to keep them out altogether; in others whites banded together to drive them away by force. Racially motivated rioting erupted in many cities, feeding the hostility and distrust between white and black people that encouraged racial separation.

Urban segregation had existed during the 19th century, but it had affected only the small minority of blacks living outside of rural areas. The rapid movement of African Americans into both Northern and Southern cities made the new century an era of large-scale urban segregation. At the mercy of white landlords, newly urbanized blacks found their choices about where to live tightly restricted. Some municipalities further limited their choices by enacting ordinances that designated exactly where black and white people could live.

The first city to pass a residential segregation ordinance was San Francisco, in 1890. This law forced Chinese residents to relocate. A local court quickly overturned the law, however, ruling it a violation of the Fourteenth Amendment's equal protection clause. Two decades later segregation ordinances targeting African Americans were enacted in such Southern cities as Atlanta, Georgia; Baltimore, Maryland; Louisville, Kentucky; and Richmond, Virginia. These laws took various forms, but all rested on the pretext that they eased race relations. A Virginia statute authorizing municipal segregation laws was clear on this point:

> Whereas the preservation of the public morals, public health and public order in the cities and towns of this commonwealth is endangered by the residence of white and colored people in close proximity to one another . . .

The question of whether municipal segregation laws were constitutional reached the U.S. Supreme

---

Some of the parks have signs, "No Negroes allowed on these grounds except as servants." Pitiful, pitiful customs and laws that make war on women and babes!

◆

—Letter of a black mother to the *Independent*, September 18, 1902

Court in 1915 in a case originating in Louisville, Kentucky, where a white resident had violated local law by selling his property to an African American. Citing the same Fourteenth Amendment principle that had been invoked in San Francisco, the Supreme Court ruled Louisville's law unconstitutional, because it represented a state's denying due process to citizens by restricting their right to sell their own property. This decision prompted many cities to redraft their own segregation laws to make them constitutionally acceptable, but the Supreme Court effectively abolished all state-imposed residential segregation in another case, *Buchanan v. Warley*, in 1917.

As cities futilely sought ways of circumventing the *Buchanan* decision, a new, unofficial technique of segregating neighborhoods spread throughout the country. White property owners began writing private contracts known as "restrictive covenants," which were designed to keep African Americans and other racial and ethnic minorities out of their neighborhoods. Buyers who signed these covenants pledged never to sell or rent their property to members of whatever groups the covenants designated as undesirable. Such agreements were often written into deeds, thereby forcing buyers to endorse segregation whether they personally favored it or not.

Although restrictive covenants were essentially private agreements, their enforcement relied upon government courts. When a constitutional challenge to covenants reached the Supreme Court in 1926, in *Corrigan and Curtis v. Buckley*, the Court ruled that covenants did not violate the Fourteenth Amendment because they were private—not state—actions. Until the Supreme Court tightened its rulings against restrictive covenants in 1948, such agreements would play a major role in fostering urban segregation.

Confined by both law and developing custom, African-American neighborhoods invariably became congested. Their residents suffered all the conditions normally accom-

Residential segregation was one of the main problems facing African Americans who poured into cities during the early 20th century. (Courtesy Library of Congress, Prints and Photographs Division)

panying overcrowding and poverty: limited services, health problems, high crime rates, and juvenile delinquency. Moreover, residential segregation strengthened other forms of segregation. Local schools in almost every city were segregated in fact, if not in law. Churches—which like schools were typically based in neighborhoods—remained rigidly segregated. Equally important, residential segregation reinforced psychological separation among the races by fostering the idea that each group "belongs" in its own place.

In 1901 the leading black spokesperson was Booker T. Washington. However, although many blacks endorsed his renunciation of social and political equality in favor of industrial education and racial uplifting, not all agreed with him. A growing number preferred the goals of W. E. B. Du Bois, who wanted nothing less than full political rights and an end to all forms of segregation. In 1905 Du Bois and other young black intellectuals leaders met at Niagara Falls, on the U.S.–Canada border—which had been the terminus of the abolitionists' Underground Railroad—to launch an organization that would aggressively fight against discrimination. The Niagara Movement that they founded unabashedly criticized white discrimination.

Through these years racially motivated lynchings increased throughout the South, but the attention of white Northerners was not fully caught until race rioting erupted in 1908 in Abraham Lincoln's hometown, Springfield, Illinois. This shocking event spurred the formation of a new interracial organization to fight for black equality. On Lincoln's 100th birthday the following year, black and white leaders met in New York City to found the National Association for the Advancement of

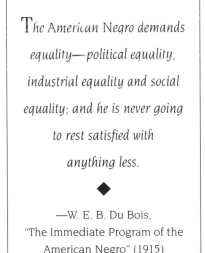

The American Negro demands equality—political equality, industrial equality and social equality; and he is never going to rest satisfied with anything less.

◆

—W. E. B. Du Bois,
"The Immediate Program of the American Negro" (1915)

Colored People (NAACP). When this organization was officially established in 1910, it absorbed the Niagara Movement and made Du Bois its director of publicity and research.

The NAACP aimed for complete abolition of legal segregation, implementation of all citizenship and voting rights conferred by the Fourteenth and Fifteenth Amendments, equal education for all children, and an end to racial violence. A legal redress committee was formed to investigate rights violations, and Du Bois went to work editing the *Crisis*, a magazine that publicized the association's work. After Booker T. Washington's death in 1915, Du Bois emerged as the most influential spokesperson for African-American rights.

Another civil rights organization that formed in New York City in 1910 was the National Urban League. Originally called the National League on Urban Conditions Among Negroes, this body worked to help blacks migrating from the South to adjust to the special problems of living in Northern cities. Through its first three decades the league worked to improve housing and employment conditions for African Americans and lobbied against discriminatory government policies.

As the NAACP, Urban League, and other civil rights organizations began campaigning against discrimination, new efforts to curtail black rights were arising in unexpected places. In 1913 members of Congress were busy introducing racially discriminatory legislation—including many measures calling for segregation in the District of Columbia, the only part of the United States over which the federal government had direct authority. Most of the proposed discriminatory bills were never enacted; however, shortly after President Woodrow Wilson was inaugurated, he issued an executive order segregating the dining rooms and restrooms used by federal civil servants in Washington, D.C. It would take a quarter of a century to remove Jim Crow arrangements from federal buildings.

America's entry into the First World War marked another turning point in the condition of African Americans. On the eve of the war, less than three percent of the 750,000 men on active duty in the army and National Guard were black. When the United States finally entered the war in April 1917, blacks responded eagerly to the call for arms, but recruiters were initially reluctant to accept them. By the time the war ended, however, more than 365,000 African Americans saw military service—double the number who had served in the Civil War.

Almost all these men served in the army. None were admitted to the marines, and the few accepted by the navy were mostly restricted to menial, nonmilitary tasks. Black recruits in the army encountered segregation almost every-where—from training camps to combat duty. Black soldiers whom the army brought into the South for training met such hostility from Southern whites that the War Department decided to train black recruits in their own home regions. The department's plan to create an all-black army division—the 92nd—was nearly frustrated by its inability to set up a segregated training base big enough to accommodate an entire division. Instead, soldiers of the 92nd trained at camps scattered between Illinois and New York, and they did not even assemble as one division until they reached Europe.

An intensive black lobbying effort persuaded the War Department to commission black officers, but the army insisted on maintaining segregated training camps. Many African-American leaders objected to Jim Crow camps on principle, but most decided that this unprecedented chance to create a corps of black officers was too valuable to jeopardize by insisting on integration. Eventually the army set up a black officer-training camp in Iowa.

African Americans played a disproportionate role in the European theater of the war, where they were among the first American troops to arrive. Black battalions landed most of the U.S. troops and supplies and helped prepare American forces for combat in France. The first black combat troops, the 93rd Division, arrived early and were attached to divisions of the French army. Several black units, notably the 369th Infantry, distinguished themselves in combat. After the 92nd Division—which had not previously trained together —reached France, it underwent additional training and did not see combat until three months before the war ended. As the only entirely African-American division fighting as a unit in the war, the 92nd became a target of German propaganda designed to demoralize black soldiers by reminding them of injustices they suffered at home.

African Americans serving in France made the pleasant discovery that not all whites were bigoted. French civilians treated them so well, in fact, that white American servicemen complained. Die-hard segregationists went so far as to engineer publication of a French military directive asking civilians to be less friendly toward black Americans.

When the war ended, black soldiers returned home hoping to be rewarded for their patriotic service with improvements in their social and economic condition. Instead they met white resentment and violence. Deteriorating economic conditions in the South during the war and the expansion of industrial jobs in the North had driven perhaps a million African Americans north in the "Great Migration." These new black migrants were met by white violence in many Northern cities. One of the worst disturbances occurred in East St. Louis, Illinois, where a factory's hiring of blacks provoked a riot that left 40 black men dead.

As black servicemen were returned to civilian life, what has been called the "Red Summer" of 1919 put cities through some of the most destructive and violent race rioting in American history. Black veterans in uniform were often among its victims. One typically ugly example of how petty breaches of segregation customs could trigger mob violence occurred in Chicago that summer. When a young black man swam into an area of Lake Michigan that whites regarded as

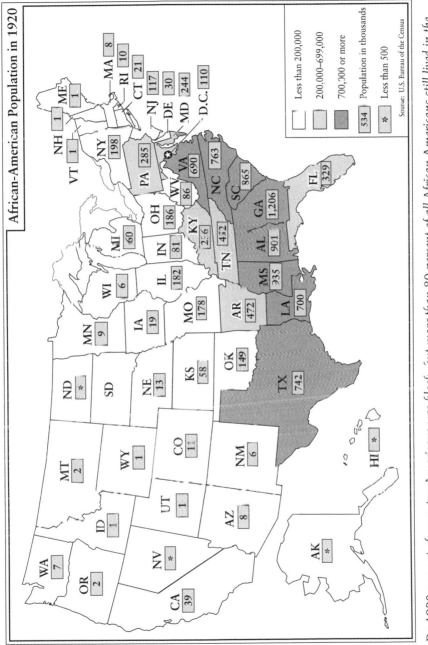

African-American Population in 1920

MT 2 | ND * | MN 9 | WI 6 | MI 60
ID 1 | SD | | IA 19 | IL 182 | IN 81 | OH 186
WY 1 | NE 13 | | | MO 178 | KY 236 | WV 86
CO 11 | KS 58 | OK 149 | | TN 452 | NC 763 | VA 690
UT 1 | | | AR 472 | MS 935 | AL 901 | GA 1,206 | SC 865
AZ 8 | NM 6 | | TX 742 | LA 700 | | | FL 329

WA 7 | OR 2 | CA 39 | NV *

NH 1 | ME 1 | MA 8 | RI 10 | CT 21 | NJ 117 | DE 30 | MD 244 | D.C. 110
VT 1 | NY 198 | PA 285

HI * | AK *

Legend:
- ☐ Less than 200,000
- ☐ 200,000–699,000
- ■ 700,300 or more
- 534 Population in thousands
- * Less than 500

Source: U.S. Bureau of the Census

By 1920 one out of every ten Americans was black, but more than 80 percent of all African Americans still lived in the South, where segregation practices were harshest.

exclusively theirs, white beachgoers threw rocks at him. The man happened to drown—perhaps accidentally—and rumors spread that he had been murdered. Soon black and white mobs were rampaging through the city. The melee lasted 13 days, killing 38 persons, injuring 537 others, and destroying the homes of more than 1,000 families—mostly blacks.

With the wartime industrial boom largely spent, urban jobs were hard to find, and overcrowding in segregated housing was worse than ever. The disappointment that black veterans felt after the war made many look for fresh alternatives to better their condition. With the demand for information greater than ever, newspapers written by and for African Americans sprang up in almost every sizable black community. Papers such as the *Chicago Defender, Baltimore Afro-American, New York Age*, and *Pittsburgh Courier* joined the voices calling attention to injustice and demanding full rights for African Americans.

One of the most popular black movements of the postwar years, Marcus Garvey's Universal Negro Improvement Association (UNIA), published a popular weekly newspaper, the *Negro World*. Through its newspaper and hundreds of branch chapters, the UNIA advocated black economic independence and racial separatism instead of the political and social equality sought by the NAACP and other organizations. Garvey argued that there was no point in striving for integration. Not only was such a quest futile, he asserted, but the quest itself reinforced false beliefs that success for blacks lay only in emulating whites.

Part of Garvey's program was a throwback to the relocation schemes of the abolitionist era. He called for "redeeming" Africa—most of which was then under European colonial rule—and building a United States of Africa in which blacks from all over the world would rule themselves. In 1920 the UNIA convened a world conference in the Harlem section of New York City, that proclaimed Garvey "provisional president of Africa." To foster trade, travel, and communications among the world's scattered black peoples, Garvey also organized the Black Star Line—the first shipping company owned by African Americans. Garvey's "back-to-Africa" movement ultimately settled a handful of people in independent Liberia, but otherwise accomplished little. By the mid-1920s it was essentially dead. Nevertheless, the movement left a legacy of black pride and distrust of integration on which modern black nationalist movements later drew to challenge the very idea of integration.

Meanwhile, the NAACP was intensifying its campaign for promoting African-American political equality, leaving economic issues for the future. The organization soon demonstrated that its most important work would be in waging legal battles against discrimination. During its first decades it won three major legal cases, including the Supreme Court's 1917 *Buchanan v. Warley* decision, which nullified residential segregation ordinances. Two years earlier, in *Guinn v. United States*, an NAACP suit led the Supreme Court to invoke the Fifteenth Amendment to invalidate grandfather clauses in Maryland and Oklahoma voting laws. In *Moore v. Dempsey* in 1923, the Court ordered the retrial of an African American convicted of murder in Arkansas because he had been tried by an all-white jury.

Buoyed by these legal successes, the NAACP broadened its attacks on the separate-but-equal doctrine. However, not all its challenges succeeded. For example, one of its suits against restrictive covenants led to the Supreme Court's upholding of their constitutionality in *Corrigan and Curtis v. Buckley* in 1926. The following year, however, an NAACP challenge to all-white primary elections, in *Nixon v. Condon*, forced Texas to admit black voters to its state primaries.

The Depression of the 1930s hurt the entire country, but it was especially hard on blacks, most of whom were at the lowest economic level. Although widespread hard times did not discriminate between black and white sufferers, relief workers occasionally did. Religious and charitable services in some communities refused to assist African Americans.

Many federal government relief programs benefitted blacks greatly, but even they were not without elements of segregation. For example, camps of the Civilian Conservation Corps (CCC)—which provided paying jobs and training for young males—were rigidly segregated. The federal Works Progress Administration (WPA) projects subsidized the construction of hospitals and public buildings, some of which were intended primarily for African-American communities. Federal contracts for projects in black communities generally called for hiring African-American construction workers. Such provisions were often ignored, however, creating the occasional spectacle of all-white crews building facilities in all-black neighborhoods.

The plight of black workers was made tougher because they were long excluded from most labor unions. In 1925, however, African Americans made an important advance when A. Philip Randolph organized the Brotherhood of Sleeping Car Porters and Maids. With support from the NAACP, National Urban League, and American Federation of Labor, the new union won a tough struggle for recognition from the Pullman Company a dozen years later. Although the union had only 8,000 members, its key position within the vital rail transportation industry gave it a disproportionate voice in the growing African-American struggle for equality.

As the Depression years drew to a close, a new spirit of hope was in the

> *Wartime segregation in the armed forces is another instance of how a social pattern may wreak moral havoc. Practically all white officers and enlisted men in all branches of service saw Negro military personnel performing only the most menial functions. They saw Negroes recruited for the common defense treated as men apart and distinct from themselves.*
>
> ◆
>
> —To Secure These Rights
> (1947)

air. It was dramatized by a blow to segregation that was struck in 1939, when the great black contralto Marian Anderson returned from a triumphant European tour and applied to sing at Constitution Hall in Washington, D.C. After the all-white Daughters of the American Revolution rejected her request, Eleanor Roosevelt—the wife of President Franklin D. Roosevelt—resigned from the organization in protest. Secretary of the Interior Harold L. Ickes then invited Anderson to sing at the Lincoln Memorial, where she performed before 75,000 people on Easter Day.

Around this same time events outside of the United States were moving the world toward another great war. By the end of 1939 war had erupted in Europe and East Asia. At that time the U.S. military had reached its lowest ebb, with the army shrinking to only 230,000 men, 5,000 of whom were African Americans—including just 12 officers. The War Department was anxious to activate more units, so Congress passed a selective service act to begin drafting men. In contrast to past laws, this one forbade racial discrimination, but many local draft boards nevertheless discriminated against blacks. African Americans wasted no time in protesting.

In September 1940 A. Philip Randolph and other leaders presented a list of demands to President Roosevelt calling for fairer treatment of African Americans in the military and in the federal government generally. The demands included nondiscrimination in military training, assignments, and promotion, and more positions for black civilians in the War Department. The department promised to recruit African Americans into the military in proportion to their numbers in the country at large and took steps to increase black representation in civilian jobs, but it did nothing to demonstrate that it would discontinue its policy of maintaining separate white and black armies.

In late 1940 the War Department announced the creation of a program to train black pilots at Tuskegee, Alabama. As when the department had set up a special black training camp for officers during the First World War, many African Americans protested this new proposal for segregation. Others, however, welcomed this opportunity for black pilots, despite its Jim Crow conditions. About 600 black pilots eventually qualified. Aside from the air corps, the War Department integrated its officer training facilities, which eventually commissioned several thousand black officers.

Meanwhile, as the defense industries were increasing production, Randolph and other black labor leaders grew impatient with the lack of progress in hiring African Americans. Frustrated by federal government's disinterest in this discrimination, Randolph proposed, in January 1941, that 100,000 blacks should march on Washington, D.C., to com-

These black troops waiting to be shipped to Europe were among nearly a half million African Americans who served overseas during World War II. (Courtesy Library of Congress, Prints and Photographs Division)

mand the nation's attention. Evidence of widespread support for this idea moved President Roosevelt personally to confer with Randolph and other black leaders several times during the summer. He appealed to them not to conduct their march, but they refused until he promised to issue an executive order "with teeth in it," forbidding discrimination in either government services or defense industries with federal contracts. A month later Roosevelt established the Fair Employment Practices Commission to monitor compliance with his order. There was considerable defiance of the order, especially in the South, but it nevertheless helped many African Americans to get jobs they might otherwise not have had.

After Japan's December 7 attack on Pearl Harbor pulled the United States into the war at the end of 1941, the navy eased some of its discriminatory recruiting policies. Nevertheless, it set up a separate training camp for black recruits. The Navy Department simultaneously opened the Marine Corps to African-American recruits for the first time ever. By 1944 black sailors were serving in all the naval ratings, and the navy was commissioning black officers for the first time.

Eventually nearly 1 million African Americans—men and women—served in the armed forces. Roughly 700,000 were in the army, another 165,000 in the navy, 17,000 in the marines, and 5,000 in the Coast Guard. Of the million African Americans who saw military service during World War II, about half went overseas. Until near the end of the war, most black army men served in segregated units. As in World War I, black units played a disproportionate role in the transportation and engineering corps in the European theater of the war. This time, however, 22 all-black combat units fought in Europe, including the reactivated 92nd Division. Black air-corps pilots who had trained at Tuskegee served throughout Europe, particularly in the Mediterranean region, and performed especially valuable service in bomber escort duty.

In contrast to earlier eras, black servicemen were far less willing to tolerate discriminatory treatment. Much of the discrimination that they experienced occurred on American soil. Segregation was practiced on many military bases, particularly in the South, where exchanges, entertainment facilities, and transportation services were typically segregated. Jackie Robinson, who later became famous in major league baseball, typified the new attitude among black soldiers by refusing to heed the Jim Crow seating arrangements on a bus—an act of disobedience for which he was court-martialed. In response to persistent complaints, the War Department ordered an end to racial segregation in all military transportation and recreation facilities in July 1944.

As during the previous world war, the expansion of wartime industries sparked large-scale black migration to the North. The massive influx of Southern blacks into Northern cities renewed racial tensions and violence. Detroit, for example, experienced one of the most destructive race riots in American history during the summer of 1943. Black servicemen, even in uniform, were often treated roughly away from their military bases. Some movie theaters and restaurants in Northern towns refused them admission, and some Southern restaurants went so far as to treat enemy prisoners better than their African-American guards. Support bodies, such as the United Services Organization (USO), had mixed policies. Most USO clubs in the North were integrated, while those in the South were segregated.

At the time the United States entered the war, the battle against segregation was mounting at home. In April 1941 the Supreme Court ruled that separate railway-car facilities must be substantially equal in a case brought by a Northern black congressman, Arthur W. Mitchell, who did not like the treatment he received while traveling in the South. The following year 50 young blacks founded the Congress of Racial Equality (CORE) to mount nonviolent direct-action campaigns against racial discrimination. Interracial groups, such as the Southern Region Council, began forming throughout the South, seeking ways to combat race prejudice and discrimination.

In 1946 the Supreme Court outlawed segregation on all interstate bus transportation in *Morgan v. Virginia,* a case arising from a black woman's refusal to sit in the back of a Jim Crow bus traveling from Virginia to Maryland. The ruling had little immediate effect on the South, but it pointed the way for further challenges to segregation. The following year, CORE tested the decision by sending "freedom riders" on buses entering the South—using a tactic that it would employ with greater effect during the early 1960s. Throughout these years the NAACP continued its legal war against voting discrimination. In 1944 its efforts were rewarded when the Supreme Court passed down a decision that overturned all-white primary elections in *Smith v. Allwright.*

In December 1946 President Harry S Truman appointed a national committee to study the state of civil rights in the country and make recommendations. The committee issued its report in the fall of 1947, strongly condemning racial injustice and calling for programs to end segregation. The following year the president appointed another committee to study ways to desegregate the armed forces. In July he took direct action by issuing an executive order that unequivocally banned segregation throughout the military and called for an end to discrimination in federal employment generally.

Professional sports were also beginning to change around this time. In April 1947 Jackie Robinson became the first black major-league baseball player in modern times. After having spent a season on a minor-league team in Montreal, Canada, Robinson ignored white taunting and threats during his first major-league season and won rookie-of-the-year honors and helped the Brooklyn Dodgers win the pennant. Soon other teams began signing black players to their rosters. By 1959 every major-league team was integrated. Outside the world of sports, baseball's integration had little direct

After World War II ended, African Americans lobbied for complete desegregation of the armed forces. In July 1948 demonstrators picketing the Democratic National Convention carried signs demanding an executive order that would outlaw military segregation. Two weeks after President Harry S Truman won the party's nomination he issued just such an order.   (Courtesy Library of Congress, Prints and Photographs Division)

impact. However, the highly visible accomplishments of Robinson and other black athletes helped pave the way for public acceptance of desegregation in other fields.

The year after Robinson broke the color line in baseball, another challenge to housing segregation reached the Supreme Court. At issue in the case of *Shelley v. Kraemer* was not whether private property sellers had the right to make buyers sign restrictive covenants, but whether government courts should hear suits against people who violated such covenants. Citing the equal protection clause of the Fourteenth Amendment, the Supreme Court ruled that "the coercive power of government" was not to be used to enforce segregation. Without the support of the courts, restrictive covenants ceased to have any legal weight.

As these and other promising developments unfolded, a quiet battle was being waged in the courts to desegregate education. After the collapse of Reconstruction in the 19th century every Southern state, as well as most border states, had legislated racially separate school systems. Segregated schools were universal in the South by 1900. Some Northern states, such as Arizona, Illinois, Indiana, Kansas, New Jersey, and Ohio, also sanctioned segregation in some school districts, but they were exceptions—just as New York was another kind of exception in explicitly prohibiting separate schools in 1900. Although most Northern states did not officially sanction segregated schools, residential segregation in Northern cities ensured that most Northern schools remained segregated as well.

Although the Supreme Court's 1896 *Plessy v. Ferguson* decision had no direct bearing on education, its separate-but-equal doctrine was used to justify school segregation throughout the South. During the first half of the 20th century every Southern state's school system was officially and rigidly segregated. Under the separate-but-equal doctrine it was presumed that black schools were "equal" to those of whites, but this was never the case. By every objective measure—buildings, books, equipment, teacher salaries—black schools were demonstrably inferior. The differences could be measured in the money that states spent on their schools. In 1900 Southern states spent 50 percent more per pupil on white schools than they did on black schools. Over the next several decades the disparity grew larger. By the late 1930s Southern states were spending three times more per pupil on white schools.

Despite such obvious gross disparities between black and white schools, the NAACP refrained from challenging public-school segregation until the 1950s. In the meantime it mounted a methodical campaign against segregation in higher education, which it rightly judged to be vulnerable to legal challenges under the separate-but-equal doctrine.

The Southern states had also created separate systems of higher education, with government-supported all-black colleges in every state. Segregationist philosophy presumed that as long as a state appeared to provide equal educational opportunities to everyone, the separate-but-equal doctrine's requirements would be met. However limited their resources, black elementary and secondary schools usually provided at least the rudiments of all the subjects appropriate to each grade level. In contrast, higher education—particularly postgraduate education—was a much different matter because of its more specialized curricula. It was impossible for a state to pretend that equality existed when it offered no training at all in law, medicine, or other professional fields to blacks. Some states tried to compensate for the deficiencies of black schools by offering students tuition scholarships to out-of-state graduate schools.

The NAACP began challenging such programs in 1933. Following a strategy devised by lawyer Charles Hamilton Houston to expose the fallacy of the separate-but-equal doctrine, NAACP lawyers scored their first victory in 1935 when they represented a black Marylander, Donald Murray, who wanted to enter the University of Maryland's law school. Future Supreme Court justice Thurgood Marshall acted as the NAACP's chief counsel. When a Maryland court of appeals accepted the NAACP argument that Maryland's out-of-state scholarship grants did not satisfy the separate-but-equal principle, the first breach in the walls of educational segregation appeared. Murray entered the University of Maryland's law school.

The next step in widening that breach came in a case arising out of a black Missourian's attempt to enter the University of Missouri's law school. The NAACP carried Lloyd Gaines's case to the U.S. Supreme Court. Writing for the majority in *Missouri ex rel. Gaines* in 1938, Chief Justice

Charles Evans Hughes ruled that each state not only had the duty to provide education for all its citizens but also that it must provide such education *within* its own borders. Given a choice between admitting Gaines to its white law school or building a new law school for blacks, Missouri opted for the latter. As the NAACP prepared to challenge Missouri's plan to create a Jim Crow law school, Gaines himself mysteriously disappeared. His disappearance ended the case—but not the legal precedent that the case set. Southern states were soon scrambling to make up the curriculum deficiencies at their black colleges.

In 1940 the NAACP chartered the NAACP Legal Defense and Educational Fund as a tax-exempt corporation to serve as its legal arm. Over the next decade NAACP lawyers continually challenged states that tried to satisfy the requirements of the *Gaines* decision by improvising Jim Crow educational facilities. This campaign culminated in 1950 in the case of *Sweatt v. Painter*, in which the Supreme Court ruled that Texas's hastily created black "law school" was not equal to its white law school. Moreover, the Court asserted, separate professional schools could not, by their nature, be equal. Each such court decision made it clearer that "equality" was to be measured by substance, not appearance.

By 1950 repeated NAACP victories over segregation in higher education had done irreparable damage to the foundations of the separate-but-equal doctrine. The experience that the organization gained in this process and the constitutional principles that it forced the courts to articulate laid a solid basis for an even greater desegregation challenge in the second half of the century: the fight against public school segregation.

NOTE

p. 120 "Whereas the preservation . . ." quoted in Charles S. Johnson, *Background to Patterns of Negro Segregation* (New York: Crowell, 1970), p. 175.

9

The Modern
Civil Rights Era

American contributions to the Allied victory in World War II left the United States the unchallenged leader of the *"free world"*—the postwar term for the noncommunist nations outside of the Soviet and Chinese blocs. World events of the ensuing decades made Americans increasingly aware of their special role as an international model of democracy. Cold War rivals were quick to call attention to lynchings, racial discrimination, and any other evidence that American democracy was imperfect. Growing sensitivity to the fact that racial discrimination was incompatible with democratic ideals did much to prepare Americans to accept the profound changes in the social and political condition of African Americans that were to come.

And many were these changes. The 1950s and 1960s advanced the process of desegregation further than it had gone in the previous century. Credit for these advances goes to the inherent color-blindness of the U.S. Constitution and the unwillingness of African Americans to accept anything less than full citizenship. The antisegregation work painstakingly done in previous decades began to bear fruit; the legal struggle waged by the NAACP had worked so many cracks in the walls of segregation that it seemed that only a few more well-placed blows would cause the entire edifice to crumble.

Several such blows came during the mid-1950s. In 1954 the U.S. Supreme Court issued one of the most important rulings in its history when it unanimously struck down the principle of separate-but-equal public schools in *Brown v. Board of Education of Topeka, Kansas*. Although this decision applied directly only to public schools, its ringing condemnation of the logic of separating people by race turned the tide irrevocably against legal segregation in all its manifestations. The *Brown* decision created a strong constitutional argument against segregation, but nothing changed automatically—even in the schools directly affected by the decision. African Americans had to fight harder than ever before to force change, while segregationists scrambled to find new methods of maintaining racial segregation. The important change was that blacks now knew that they had the Constitution fully behind them. Once it was clear that segregation was not impervious to attack, a new era of direct action began in which African Americans—with white support—organized marches, boycotts, sit-ins, and other protests that confronted segregation head on.

The year after the *Brown* decision, a black Alabama woman, Rosa Parks, refused to give up her bus seat to a white man. Her arrest for violating a Jim Crow law touched off a successful protest movement that helped launch the modern

Jim Crow at Mid-Century_____

Gwendolyn L. Rosemond, a college professor in New England, recalls what it was like to travel in the South around 1950, when she accompanied her mother on trips to South Carolina.

> We change trains in Cincinnati, Mama and I, and board the Carolina Special. All the way there, and for weeks before we begin the trip, she admonishes me.
> "At Cincinnati we head South, into Jim Crow country. You say 'ma'm' and 'sir' if anybody white says anything to you."
> Something is unspoken. What will happen if I don't?
> From Columbus to Cincinnati white people share our coach. From Cincinnati, where we cross the Ohio, the only white person to pass through is the conductor. Although he and the porter both wear uniforms (though not identical), I can tell the conductor from the porter. The conductor is white and takes our tickets. He never speaks. The porter is black, carries our baggage, smiles, and flirts with Mama. When Mama wants to know anything, she asks the porter.
> Mama says, "They always put the colored coach up front, nearest the engine. That way we get the smoke and cinders and the white folks don't."
> The day before we leave, Mama fries chicken, bakes plain cake, makes bread and butter sandwiches, and packs our meals for the trip. The dining car is for white folks only, but whatever they have there is not as sweet and peppery and fresh as Mama's day-old fried chicken, washed down with icy water from the fountain in a tiny paper cone.
> In Spartanburg, Auntie meets the train. A bustling, fair-skinned, no-nonsense woman, she hustles us into an ancient waiting cab. Year after year, the driver is always black, even though shinier and newer cabs with white drivers stand nearby. Auntie averts her eyes from them, not in a humble way; they just aren't there in her vision. No, I cannot stop for a drink or go to the rest room; we'll be at Auntie's momentarily. I wait. I know that the water in the verboten white fountain is sweet and cold and pure and clear. That in the colored fountain is not. Only in the most dire and potentially embarrassing emergency will Mama relinquish her fragile power over custom and permit use of the colored facilities.

We make Auntie's our base from which we travel by bus or by car to family not accessible by train. On the bus we sit in the rear, or stand, or crouch upon our luggage. Air conditioning is not yet a standard feature; open windows bring exhaust fumes and dust, humidity and dirt. At rest stops we grab a Coke from an outside window. Mama breaks out the ubiquitous fried chicken. Traveling by car for any long distance requires two drivers to relieve one another. The vacancy sign in the motel or hotel means "white only." We drive day and night, virtually non-stop. During the day, we stop briefly at dingy, filthy rest rooms marked just for us. Mama carries Kleenex; we develop strong bladders. At night, the men drive, the children sleep, the women keep watch, praying silently.

From Auntie's we journey "down home," into the country. Usually my uncle drives, having arrived from Cleveland in his Chrysler New Yorker. His Ohio license plate brands him as a Northerner, the car as an "uppity negro." If his son drives, my uncle nags him all the way.

"Don't call attention to yourself. You want to land in a cracker jail, or worse?"

Or worse. The phrase hangs over every thought, every word, every gesture. In this year, *Brown v. the Board of Education* is inconceivable; "civil rights" is not yet a phrase; Emmett Till* is not yet dead. Late one night, in the rain and fog, another uncle is stopped for speeding. We follow the county sheriff's car to somewhere, in heavy and absolute silence. The joyous return from a full day at church vanishes, vanquished by palpable fear. Even Auntie is subdued. The uncle returns to the car, humiliated, poorer, but he escapes the "or worse."

One year, Mama and I begin our trip under unusually worrisome circumstances.

"They say in the news that colored and white can ride on the same coach on the train. But I doubt if it's really true."

At Cincinnati I rehearse my ma'ms and sirs and we board the old Carolina Special. The conductor directs us to our coach. White people get on our coach; they sit down. They look at us; we look out the window. Mama tenses. Finally, the porter comes through.

"Are we in the right car?" Mama whispers.

He nods. I don't think he believes it either.

On our next trip we eat in the dining car; we do not order fried chicken. ◆

* A black teenager lynched in Mississippi in 1955 for speaking to a white woman, Emmett Till became a symbol of racial injustice in the South.

civil rights movement and elevate Martin Luther King, Jr., to national leadership. Hundreds of thousands of black and white people took part in the new civil rights movement. Individuals, groups, and both old and new civil rights organizations aggressively attacked segregation and other forms of racial discrimination everywhere they found them. By the mid-1960s few bastions of segregation were left.

After President Harry S Truman ordered an end to segregation in the military in 1948, the armed services moved quickly to comply. U.S. involvement in the Korean War during the early 1950s gave the military an added incentive to desegregate, to avoid the embarrassment of posing as champions of the free world while fighting against Asians with separate black and white units. In 1954, a year after this war ended, the Defense Department announced that its last "all-Negro" units had been disbanded. When the United States entered the Vietnam War a decade later, all its military forces were thoroughly integrated. (Later still, when the United States fought in the Gulf War in 1991, the nation's highest ranking military officer was an African American, General Colin Powell, the chairman of the Joint Chiefs of Staff.)

At mid-century the separate-but-equal doctrine that had emerged from the Supreme Court's 1896 *Plessy v. Ferguson* decision still buttressed widespread segregation, particularly in the South. What appealed to segregationists about the phrase "*separate but equal*" was the word *separate*. In contrast, African Americans focused on *equal*; the *Plessy* decision did, after all, imply that everyone had a right to equality. The key question throughout the 20th-century legal battle against segregation, however, was whether "separate but equal" was even possible. By temporarily conceding that *Plessy* might have made segregation constitutional, the NAACP lawyers concentrated their legal assault on the inequalities associated with segregation. Then by proving that equality could *not* be compatible with separation, they led the Supreme Court to rule that segregation itself was unconstitutional.

The legal campaign leading up to the Supreme Court's landmark *Brown* decision in 1954 began indirectly, starting with the NAACP suits against university graduate schools during the 1930s. The NAACP launched a *direct* legal assault on public school segregation in mid-1951 by bringing suit against schools in South Carolina. That case, *Briggs v. Elliott*, reached a federal court in South Carolina that ruled that segregation was not necessarily a form of discrimination. After the NAACP appealed that decision, the *Briggs* case was combined with others from Kansas, Delaware, Virginia, and the District of Columbia under the collective name *Brown et al. v. Board of Education of Topeka, Kansas, et al.* (This name was used because the *Brown* case had appeared first alphabetically on the Court's October 1953 docket.)

All these cases involved the refusal of school districts to admit black students to white schools. The Kansas case had originated in 1951 in Topeka, where the daughter of a black clergyman was denied admission to the school nearest to her home. When the father sued on her behalf, a U.S. district court ruled that segregation could have a "detrimental effect" on black children by contributing to "a sense of inferiority," but it refused to provide relief.

Thurgood Marshall, again acting as the NAACP's chief legal counsel, filed a brief before the Supreme Court laying out the argument that racially based discrimination in public schools violated the Fourteenth Amendment. This brief specifically challenged *Plessy*'s separate but equal doctrine:

> Candor requires recognition that the plain purpose and effect of segregated education is to perpetuate an inferior status for Negroes which is America's sorry heritage from slavery. But the primary purpose of the Fourteenth Amendment was to deprive the states of *all* power to perpetuate a caste system.

The timing of these cases was fortunate, because they reached the Supreme Court shortly after President Dwight D. Eisenhower appointed Earl Warren chief justice of the United States in 1953. Warren came to the Court with strong moral objections to segregation, and he convinced his fellow justices of the necessity of their ruling unanimously against segregation, so that no one could misinterpret their decision.

On May 17, 1954, the Supreme Court ruled unanimously that *all* state-imposed school segregation was unconstitutional under the equal protection clause of the Fourteenth Amendment. Warren's summation described racially segregated schools as "inherently unequal." The separation of school children solely on the basis of race, he asserted, "generates a feeling of inferiority as to their status in the community that may affect their hearts and minds in a way unlikely ever to be undone." It was an assertion to which no honest rebuttal was possible.

The *Brown* decision applied to the four cases originating in states. The fifth, *Bolling v. Sharpe*, concerned the District of Columbia—a federally administered territory not subject to the Fourteenth Amendment's equal protection clause. Nevertheless, the Court reached the same decision in this case by invoking the Fifth Amendment's due process clause. *Bolling* was crucial to the school segregation cases because the Court could not easily outlaw school segregation in the states while permitting it in the nation's capital.

At the time of the *Brown* decision, it was estimated that unprecedented numbers of people would potentially be affected by the court order—more than 10 million children in 50,000 schools. However, despite the decision's broad application and unequivocal language, it produced little immediate change. It lacked a clear enforcement directive and it met fierce resistance from Southern whites, who dubbed May 17 "Black Monday." In 1956, 90 Southern Congressmen signed a document known as the "Southern Manifesto," accusing the Supreme Court of illegally legislating social change. In a throwback to the South's pre–Civil War resistance to the federal government, several state legislatures passed resolutions rejecting federal authority over segregation.

A year after *Brown*, the Supreme Court handed down another decision ("*Brown II*") ordering that the districts named in the original suits desegregate their schools "with all deliberate speed." Meanwhile, Southern state governments were reaching new levels of creativity in finding ways to avoid desegregating their schools. White citizens formed new organizations to combat segregation, such as "White Citizens' Councils" and the "National Association for the Advancement of White People." Racial violence again became common, and violence and intimidation were used against both white and black proponents of desegregation. A decade after *Brown* it was estimated that barely 2 percent of 3 million school-age African Americans in the South attended desegregated schools.

The strong resistance of whites to integrating schools was a measure of the importance of education in race relations. So long as African Americans were denied equal educational opportunities, the myth of black inferiority would be easier to maintain. A notorious example of the lengths to which whites went to avoid desegregation was Virginia's Prince Edward County— one of the targets of the original *Brown* cases. The response of its school board to desegregation had been to shut down the public schools completely in the early 1960s. White children attended an allegedly private school, which was actually publicly financed, while the county's black children attended no schools at all. This situation led to yet another legal challenge reaching the Supreme Court, which ordered the school board to reopen its public schools to all children in the county.

Many states put off integrating their schools by adopting clever legal stratagems to confuse the issue and cause delays. In most of these states open conflicts were avoided, so it was a surprise when one of the most dramatic confrontations in

A *defining moment in the struggle to desegregate public schools came in September 1957, when President Eisenhower sent federal troops into Little Rock, Arkansas, to enforce the integration of Central High School. This action, along with Congress's passage of the first federal civil rights act since 1875 a month earlier, demonstrated that all three branches of the federal government were committed to desegregation.* (Courtesy Library of Congress, Prints and Photographs Division)

the history of federal-state relations erupted in Little Rock, Arkansas, in the fall of 1957. After the local school worked out a plan to integrate the city's public schools, nine black students attempted to enroll in Central High School. Before they could do so, however, Governor Orval Faubus called out the National Guard to block their entry. Faced with so blatant a flouting of a federal court order, President Dwight D. Eisenhower sent federal troops into the city to enforce the school's integration.

Although the use of federal troops in Little Rock did not end resistance to school integration, it provided convincing evidence that not only the federal court system but the presidency was behind desegregation. A major part of the reason lay in the president's concern about the damage that the incident did to the nation "in the eyes of the world."

Meanwhile, the legal victories that the NAACP had won against segregation in postgraduate education during the 1930s and 1940s had not ended discrimination in higher education. The University of Oklahoma, for example, had reluctantly admitted African Americans to its graduate school in the late 1940s, but afterward used every means it could to segregate them from white students in classrooms, dining rooms, and even libraries. Such discriminatory treatment did not go unchallenged, however, and the case of *McLaurin v. Oklahoma State Regents* in 1950 resulted in the

After nine years in the air force, James Meredith decided to make a personal contribution to ending segregation at the University of Mississippi in his home state. With the support of the NAACP's legal arm, he applied to the university in 1961. After being rejected, he filed a class-action suit in federal court charging that the university's entrance requirements were discriminatory. The following year an appeals court accepted his argument and ordered the university to admit him. It took an army of federal troops to protect Meredith, but he succeeded in enrolling in October 1962 and graduated a year later. (Courtesy Library of Congress, Prints and Photographs Division)

U.S. Supreme Court's ordering the university to stop such behavior.

In September 1962 Supreme Court justice Hugo Black issued a ruling ordering the University of Mississippi to admit James H. Meredith. Mississippi governor Ross Barnett personally intervened to prevent Meredith's enrollment, but President John F. Kennedy publicly demanded that the state comply with the federal court order. Rioting broke out in Oxford, Mississippi, but federal marshals eventually were sent there to escort Meredith onto the campus. He succeeded in registering, and a year later he became the first African American to graduate from the university. The following year President John Kennedy intervened in a similar confrontation when Alabama governor George Wallace tried to prevent the integration of the University of Alabama.

In a major civil rights address delivered to the nation on June 11, 1963, President Kennedy expressed the argument for desegregation as a moral issue:

> It ought to be possible for American students of any color to attend any public institution they selected without having to be backed up by troops. It ought to be possible for American consumers of any color to receive equal service in places of public accommodation, such as hotels and restaurants, and theaters and retail stores without being forced to resort to demonstrations in the street.
>
> And it ought to be possible for American citizens of any color to register and vote in a free election without interference or fear of reprisal. . . .
>
> We are confronted primarily with a moral issue. It is as clear as the American Constitution. The heart of the question is whether all Americans are to be afforded equal rights and equal opportunities; whether we are going to treat our fellow Americans as we want to be treated. . . .
>
> We preach freedom around the world, and we mean

it. And we cherish our freedom here at home. But are we to say to the world—and much more importantly to each other—that this is the land of the free, except for the Negroes; that we have no second-class citizens, except Negroes . . .

The day after Kennedy delivered this address, Medgar Evers, the NAACP field secretary in Jackson, Mississippi, was shot dead outside his own home by a white man.

Although education had been the dominant issue in legal battles against segregation over the previous decades, it was another transportation case that led to the definitive overturning of *Plessy v. Ferguson's* separate-but-equal doctrine. That case originated in Montgomery, Alabama, whose public buses had long been segregated. In 1955 the federal Interstate Commerce Commission outlawed segregation in public conveyances traveling between states. This ruling integrated interstate (between states) transportation, but had no affect on intrastate (within states) transportation. At that time Montgomery's bus system was typical of Jim Crow buses in the South in requiring blacks, not only to sit in the rear seats, but to give up even those seats to white passengers when front rows were filled. One evening in December 1955, when seamstress Rosa Parks was riding a bus home from work, the driver ordered her to surrender her seat to a white man. Tired and fed up with such unfair treatment, Parks refused. Her subsequent arrest ignited a communitywide protest against the bus system—which was already unpopular for treating black passengers rudely. Within days a massive boycott of the buses swept through Montgomery.

Montgomery community leaders formed the Montgomery Improvement Association to coordinate the protest. Martin Luther King, Jr., who had recently become a Baptist pastor in the city, was elected to head the association. The choice was a fortunate one, as King soon proved himself a leader of outstanding ability. A disciple of the philosophy of

Indian nationalist leader Mohandas Gandhi, King believed in disciplined, nonviolent protest actions, and he helped sustain the boycotters' morale in the face of considerable adversity for nearly a year. Many people who had been dependent on buses to ride great distances to their jobs endured considerable hardships, police harassment, and threats of violence.

The lack of black riders caused Montgomery's bus system to lose money. Although the city did everything it could to force black passengers to return, the boycott maintained nearly perfect discipline through most of 1956. Meanwhile, a federal court ruled in June that Montgomery's segregated buses were unconstitutional. In November the Supreme Court upheld this decision. In the face of mounting monetary losses and the court order, the city capitulated by integrating its buses at the end of the year.

The Montgomery bus boycott was a pivotal event in the battle against segregation. It demonstrated how a well-organized and disciplined protest movement could succeed even against an entrenched white power structure. Equally important, it made civil rights protests a national issue and gave King national stature as a civil rights leader. The success of the boycott inspired protest movements in other Southern cities—including Tallahassee, Florida, where a similar bus boycott had succeeded at the same time.

Concerned about the possibility of protest movements erupting into violence, King and many of his supporters decided to form a permanent body to spread the techniques of nonviolent resistance and help communities involved in civil rights protests. In February 1957 they founded the Southern Christian Leadership Conference (SCLC) in Atlanta, Georgia, and elected King their president. Over the next decade, the SCLC moved throughout the South, helping local community leaders to organize boycotts and peaceful demonstrations. They often encountered white hostility, police harassment, jailing, and violence—most notably in

Birmingham, Alabama, where the police turned attack dogs on them in early 1963. King's unfailing adherence to his nonviolent principles through these difficult struggles led to his receiving a Nobel Peace Prize in 1964.

The decade of the 1960s was a period of rapid and revolutionary social change. It saw the convergence of the civil rights movement, a new spirit of activist change in federal government, national prosperity, and the rise of the antiwar movement. It was also a decade of charismatic leaders, notably Martin Luther King, Jr.; Malcolm X; John F. Kennedy; Robert F. Kennedy; and Lyndon B. Johnson—who did more than any previous president to promote civil rights. One of the high moments of this period occurred on August 28, 1963, when more than a ¼ million civil rights protestors converged on Washington, D.C., in a realization of the march that A. Philip Randolph had proposed back in 1941. In a moving address remembered as the "I Have a Dream" speech, Martin Luther King, Jr., summed up the aspirations for equality that African Americans held and proclaimed their urgency:

> We have waited for more than 340 year for our constitutional and God-given rights. The nations of Asia and Africa are moving with jetlike speed toward gaining political independence, but we still creep at horse-and-buggy pace toward gaining a cup of coffee at a lunch counter.
>
> ◆
>
> —Martin Luther King, Jr.,
> "Letter from Birmingham Jail,"
> April 16, 1963

It would be fatal for the nation to overlook the urgency of the moment and to underestimate the determination of the negro. This sweltering summer of the Negro's legitimate discontent will not pass until there is an invigorating autumn of freedom and equality. Nineteen-hundred and sixty-three is not an end, but a beginning. Those who hope that the Negro needed to blow off steam, and will now be content will have a rude awakening if the Nation returns to business as usual. There will neither be rest nor tranquility in America until the Negro is granted his citizenship rights.

King's speech was prophetic. The nation enjoyed little tranquility over the next decade as black demands for political and social equality intensified. King himself became a victim of the escalating social tensions when he was assassinated in 1968.

Meanwhile, one of the most remarkable aspects of the civil rights movement was the broad impact that the actions of mere handfuls of people often had. The sit-in movement is an outstanding example. In February 1960, four black college students entered a Woolworth's store in Greensboro, North Carolina. After buying a few items, they sat down at the Jim Crow lunch counter and tried to order food. After being refused service, they simply remained in their seats. Over the next few days police began arresting the demonstrators, but the lunch-counter seats were filled by other students as fast as they were taken away. Woolworth temporarily closed the store down.

The Greensboro sit-in was actually not anything new; members of CORE had staged similar sit-ins in St. Louis and Baltimore between 1949 and 1953. However, the human drama of this later protest attracted widespread news coverage. Thousands of college and high school students were soon staging similar sit-ins throughout the South. Suddenly it appeared that all it might take to bring Jim Crow businesses to a halt was the simple act of sitting down and patiently waiting to be treated fairly. The sit-in technique would soon become a major weapon

The Black Codes were a substitute for slavery; segregation was a substitute for the Black Codes; the discrimination in these sit-in cases is a relic of slavery. . . .

◆

—Supreme Court decision in *Bell v. Maryland* (1964) sit-in case in the fight against segregation. Meanwhile, these first 1960 sit-in demonstrations stimulated such a rush of college students into protest activities that the Student Non-Violent Coordinating Committee (SNCC) was formed in Raleigh, North Carolina, in April to help focus protest activities.

Another example of dramatic direct confrontation came the following year. In May 1961, 14 years after CORE had first tested the Supreme Court's ban on segregated interstate buses by sending "freedom riders" into the South, CORE resumed the tactic. During a 10-day trip from Washington, D.C., to Atlanta, Georgia, the white and black riders were repeatedly assaulted and arrested. The violence directed against subsequent riders over the next year became so intense that the federal government asked the freedom riders to stop in order to avert bloodshed. However, leaders of CORE, SNCC, and the SCLC insisted on continuing the campaign.

The dramatic antisegregation events that began in the mid-1950s helped to rouse the U.S. Congress to enact its first federal civil rights legislation since 1875. Each piece of legislation it passed between 1957 and 1968 raised the level of African-American demands and led to even more sweeping civil rights laws. The provisions of the Civil Rights Act of 1957 were concerned mainly with establishing a commission to investigate violations of existing voting laws. The law was thus more symbolic than substantive, but by virtue of passing any such legislation at all, Congress joined the judicial and executive branches of the federal government in the fight against inequality.

Congress passed the Civil Rights Act of 1960 just as a wave of sit-in demonstrations, mass marches, and other forms of protest were sweeping the South. This law—which was also known as the Voting Rights Act of 1960— strengthened federal protections of the voting rights of blacks living in the South.

The Voting Rights Commission established by the 1957 Civil Rights Act issued a formal report to the president in 1963 entitled *Freedom to the Free*. The findings of this commission stressed the critical need for even stronger federal protections of African-American voting rights. Early the following year ratification of the Twenty-fourth Amendment outlawed the use of poll taxes or other devices to deny citizens the right to vote. The amendment had a profound impact on the ability of Southern blacks to register and vote. During the following summer civil rights organizations sent hundreds of volunteers into Mississippi to help register African Americans who had never had a chance to vote. The Mississippi Freedom Summer Project produced immediate results, as thousands of black Mississippians began exercising their franchise.

A*ll persons shall be entitled to the full and equal enjoyment of the goods, services, facilities, privileges, advantages, and accommodations of any place of public accommodations of any place of public accommodation, as defined . . . without discrimination or desegregation on the ground of race, color, religion, or national origin.*

◆

—Civil Rights Act of 1964,
Title II, Section 201 (a)

The Mississippi voter registration project also contained an element of high drama when three civil rights workers—two white men and one black man—disappeared and were later found murdered. The tragedy called attention to racial violence in the South and ultimately helped to win national sympathy for the civil rights movement as a whole.

Meanwhile, Congress passed the most sweeping civil rights legislation ever proposed, the Civil Rights Act of 1964. This law outlawed discrimination in federal employment, public accommodations, transportation, and other sectors. The evident success of mass protests and direct confrontation techniques seemed to indicate that unjust laws would never again be tolerated in America. The law did not suddenly end segregation through the country; however, it did mark the final watershed by acknowledging, once and for all, that the only direction that the country could take was toward real and complete political and social equality of all its citizens.

NOTES

p. 145 "Candor requires . . ." Quoted in Blaustein and Zangrando, *Civil Rights and the Black America: A Documentary History*, p. 422.

p. 150–151 "It ought to be possible . . ." Quoted in Blaustein and Zangrando, *Civil Rights and the Black American: A Documentary History*, p. 486.

Epilogue

It would be difficult to over-state the profound nature of changes in race relations that have occurred during the second half of the 20th century. The United States still has far to go before achieving full equality for all its citizens; however, the distance that it has recently traveled has been great. Jim Crow signs have long since disappeared throughout the country, and no overtly segregationist laws remain on the books anywhere—even in the Deep South. Jim Crowism, as it was known in 1950, has vanished, almost certainly never to return.

The mid-1960s marked a watershed in the long history of the struggle against segregation in the United States. Passage of the federal civil rights acts placed all three branches of the federal government squarely against racial injustice. In addition, the long-overdue enfranchisement of black voters gave

African Americans enough real political clout to ensure that there would be no going back. These substantial achievements took much of the momentum out of the civil rights movement that had helped to bring them about by making it harder for the movement to find issues on which to focus. By the time Martin Luther King, Jr., was assassinated in 1968, the movement had crested. Arguing against the *idea* of segregation and other injustices was no longer necessary; that argument was already won.

What remained to do after the mid-1960s was ensuring that the principles of racial justice that had been won be *applied*. This required both further legislation and practical and effective enforcement of the recently passed laws. Although that struggle has continued until the present day, it has already forced virtually every government in the country to disavow segregation and other forms of racial discrimination. Three decades after passage of the major civil rights acts, overt segregation is not tolerated anywhere in public transportation, public accommodations, housing, education, employment, and other spheres. Thanks to their new voting power, African Americans are being elected in ever-increasing numbers to Congress, state legislatures, and local government offices. They are also being appointed in increasing numbers to high-level posts in the federal government, the courts, and most state and local governments.

In the ongoing struggle for equal rights public education has remained the most prominent and contentious arena— but one that has taken on new and often unexpected dimensions. During the civil rights movement the fight against segregated schools focused on the South. Since then the focus has shifted to Northern schools in which legal (*de jure*) segregation had not been an issue. This development has led to court decisions and legislation that have pulled government more fully into the fight against racial injustice. In the process it has provoked new arguments about such matters as the proper role of government in social engineering, the relationship between the federal and state governments, and what—if anything—can be done to eradicate every vestige of segregation.

As in the past the most intractable form of segregation has remained housing—thanks to residential patterns whose roots are as deep as the nation itself. Although residential segregation laws and restrictive covenants have long since disappeared, most American cities have remained racially segregated. As a result, neighborhood schools, churches, businesses, and other places that bring people together have also remained effectively segregated. In order to overcome such segregation new arguments have been articulated to justify forcing the integration of public schools by busing children among racially different neighborhoods. Through much of the 1970s and 1980s battles over the "forced busing" issue tore at the fabric of the nation's schools and threatened recent improvements in racial harmony. To avoid having their children bused into black neighborhood schools, many white families relocated or withdrew their children from public schools. Meanwhile, the benefits that African-American children were gaining from being bused into predominantly white schools were being questioned. By the 1990s busing was dying out and some black parents were beginning to raise unprecedented calls for all-black schools.

A similar controversy through this period has been a new debate over the extent to which government should go to correct racial injustices of the past by pressuring government agencies, colleges, and businesses to give African Americans preferential treatment. Programs designed to help blacks with such preferments have become known as "affirmative action." As with the debate over school busing, affirmative action policies have raised new issues and contributed their share to fostering racial animosity. Busing, affirmative action, and other new issues have ensured that the struggle over equal rights for African Americans will not soon be fully settled.

To many people—black and white—Jim Crow's disappearance, while welcome, has been only a superficial change having little to do with deeper problems of African-American poverty and other forms of racial injustice. Winning the freedom to travel on any bus or train, to dine at any restaurant, to sleep in any hotel, to enter any theater, or to attend any college has had little impact on African Americans mired in poverty in the rural South. Moreover, millions of African Americans in Northern cities still live in segregated and impoverished neighborhoods, feeling untouched by the positive changes that have taken place.

Despite these reservations, the triumph over Jim Crow may be seen as a giant step toward true equality. As long as the races were kept separate it was easy to maintain the fiction that they were fundamentally different, and that blacks were inferior. The breakdown in segregation has inevitably brought black and white people into closer and more frequent contact, helping members of both groups to shed their prejudices and misconceptions about each other. Moreover, the breakdown in segregation has helped to bring increasing numbers of blacks into more visible roles in government, business, sports, and entertainment, helping to melt away old notions about blacks' being different.

Saying farewell to Jim Crow will eventually—if not now—help to make all Americans realize that race should never be an issue in restricting anyone's rights, freedoms, or hopes.

Bibliography and Further Reading List

General Studies of Segregation

Johnson, Charles S. *Backgrounds to Patterns of Negro Segregation*. New York: Thomas Y. Crowell, 1970 (rev. ed.). Provides detailed information on the pre–civil rights era.

Kennedy, Stetson. *Jim Crow Guide to the U.S.A.: The Laws, Customs and Etiquette Governing the Conduct of Nonwhites and Other Minorities as Second-Class Citizens*. London: Lawrence & Wishart, 1959. Also available in a reprint edition, this amazing collection of segregation practices compiled by a Southern journalist is well worth examining.

Weinstein, Allen, and Frank Otto Gatell. *The Segregation Era, 1863–1954: A Modern Reader*. New York: Oxford University Press, 1970. Articles and extracts from longer works on segregation.

Woodward, C. Vann. *The Strange Career of Jim Crow*. New York: Oxford University Press, 1974 (3rd ed.). Still the best overview of American segregation, this book originated in lectures that Woodward delivered in 1954—the year of *Brown v. Board of Education*.

General Works on African-American History

Franklin, John Hope. *From Slavery to Freedom: A History of African Americans.* New York: Alfred A. Knopf, 1994 (7th ed.). Now coauthored by Alfred Moss, Jr., this elegant history is a masterful framework in which to study segregation history.

Hornsby, Alton, Jr. *The Chronology of African American History: Significant Events and People from 1619 to the Present.* Detroit: Gale, 1991. Year-by-year summary of events, with emphasis on the 20th century.

Low, W. Augustus, and Virgil A. Clift. *Encyclopedia of Black America.* New York: McGraw-Hill, 1981. An excellent one-volume reference work containing numerous entries on segregation and many other related topics.

Williams, Michael W., ed. *African American Encyclopedias.* 6 vols., New York: Marshall Cavendish, 1993; 4-vol. supplement, 1997. A comprehensive reference work designed for school libraries.

Early Nationhood

Litwack, Leon F. *North of Slavery: The Negro in the Free States, 1790–1860.* Chicago: University of Chicago Press, 1970. Traces the development of segregation in the North as a key to understanding its rise in the post–Civil War South.

Stampp, Kenneth M. *The Peculiar Institution: Slavery in the Ante-Bellum South.* 1956. New York: Vintage, 1989. A fine overview of how African Americans lived in the South under slavery.

The Civil War and Reconstruction

Fischer, Roger A. *The Segregation Struggle in Louisiana, 1862–77.* Urbana: University of Illinois Press, 1974. A brief study of the Southern state that came closest to desegregating itself during Reconstruction.

Glatthaar, Joseph T. *Forged in Battle: The Civil War Alliance of Black Soldiers and White Officers.* New York: Free Press, 1990. Detailed accounts of the famous Massachusetts 54th Infantry and other all-black units.

Voegeli, V. Jacque. *Free but Not Equal: The Midwest and the Negro During the Civil War.* Chicago: University of Chicago Press, 1970. Illuminating case study of how the Civil War gave rise to new segregation rules and exclusionary laws in one of the major regions of the North.

The Twentieth Century

Egerton, John. *Speak Now Against the Day: The Generation Before the Civil Rights Movement in the South*. New York: Alfred A. Knopf, 1994. Award-winning study of developments before the 1950s.

Myrdal, Gunnar. *An American Dilemma: The Negro Problem and Modern Democracy* (2 vols.). New York: Harper & Bros., 1944. Richly detailed source of fascinating anecdotes that examines the condition of black Americans up to the early 1940s.

The Modern Civil Rights Movement

Hampton, Henry, and Steve Fayer. *Voices of Freedom: An Oral History of the Civil Rights Movement from the 1950s through the 1980s*. New York: Bantam Books, 1990. Oral interviews collected for television's "Eyes on the Prize" project.

Kelso, Richard. *Walking for Freedom: The Montgomery Bus Boycott*. Austin, Texas: Raintree Steck-Vaughn, 1993. Narrative history.

Patterson, Charles. *The Civil Rights Movement*. New York: Facts On File, 1995. YA history of events from 1954 through 1972.

Patterson, Lillie. *Martin Luther King, Jr. and the Freedom Movement*. New York: Facts On File, 1989. A biography written for young adults.

Taylor, Branch. *Parting the Waters: America in the King Years, 1954–63*. New York: Simon & Schuster, 1989. Pulitzer Prize–winning history of the civil rights movement.

Personal Narratives

Abernathy, Ralph. *And the Walls Came Tumbling Down*. New York: Harper & Row, 1991. A vivid reconstruction of Abernathy's youth in rural Alabama and his experience as Martin Luther King, Jr.'s lieutenant during the civil rights struggle.

Beals, Melba Patitillo. *Warriors Don't Cry: A Searing Memoir of the Battle to Integrate Little Rock's Central High*. New York: Pocket Books, 1994. Memoir of one of the students who helped to integrate the Arkansas high school in 1957.

Griffin, John Howard. *Black Like Me*. New York: Signet, 1964. Poignant narrative of a white journalist who disguised himself as a black man and traveled through the Deep South.

Smith, Lillian. *Killers of the Dream*. New York: Anchor Books, 1963 (2nd ed.). Now classic memoir about life in the segregated South by a Southern white woman.

Index

Italic numbers indicate illustrations.
Cities are entered under the names of their states.